WORKPLACE ROMANCE COLLECTION

4 BOOK COLLECTION

AVALON EVERHART

Copyright © 2023 Avalon Everhart

All rights reserved.

No part of this book may be reproduced in any form by electronic or mechanical means, including information storage and retrieval systems, without permission in writing from the publisher, except by a reviewer who may quote brief passages in a review.

This is a work of fiction. Names, characters, places, and incidents either are the product of the author's imagination or are used fictitiously. Any resemblance to actual persons, living or dead, events, or locales is entirely coincidental.

1

SAVED BY HER BOSS

2

JESSICA

Work might be a shitshow, but home is even worse.

As I glance at the condescending writing on the whiteboard, I ask myself if I really want to keep living at home. I know that I'm saving money by staying with my mom, but when she writes things like, "Before you grab those chips to go with your lunch, think about what it'll feel like to be able to say what you weigh out loud and not be ashamed of the number!" Which is probably supposed to inspire me to pack some carrots instead, but I just throw in a bag of Lays potato chips in my bag and walk out the door.

Being a bigger woman has always been a crime in my household. My mom is a pilates instructor and she loves to show people the photos of her when she was pregnant with me. She might as well have been bloated from eating too many tacos at the local Mexican restaurant instead of pregnant.

Growing up with perfection like that always a few feet away didn't make me want to attain it, it made me want to go the opposite direction. Not on purpose, but that's what wound up happening. It didn't help that I was born "big-boned", as the kids say. But then puberty hit and my breasts grew and suddenly I was the talk of the town.

Mrs. Jackson might have had an enviable figure, but did you see her daughter? She had an enviable ass. And nothing made men want to have sex more than getting a glimpse at these voluptuous tits beneath a tightly fitted shirt.

Mom and I were built differently, that was for sure. That didn't necessarily mean there was anything wrong with either one of us, but I just wish she knew that I had no desire to change who I was to match her expectations.

. . .

It's motorcycle mania at work this week. As I step inside the Dirty Hands Garage, I'm accosted by the smell of grease.

"Hey, good lookin'," greets the boss and the object of my affections, Rhys. "You're wearin' the hell out of that dress, darlin'."

His green eyes look me up and down, devouring every inch of my body. As I stare at his tattooed arms peeking out beneath cut-off sleeves, I have to remind myself that he's my boss and this isn't the right place or time to be thinking the thoughts that are now going through my mind. "Morning, Rhys."

"How was the weekend, gorgeous? Do anything excitin'?" He flashes his pearly whites at me.

For a guy like Rhys, who spends his weekends riding motorcycles with his buddies or shooting pool at dirty biker bars I wouldn't have the guts to walk into, my weekend was probably boring. I spent a majority of it snuggled up with my cat watching HGTV. Nothing screams adulthood like drooling over a newly renovated kitchen and wondering if you're ever going to have the funds to have a house, let alone a kitchen that looks as nice as that.

But that's probably not what he wants to hear. He's in his 40s, he's rough around the edges, and no man with a beard like *that* wants anything to do with a woman like *me*. "Well, I mean, probably nothing exciting like you. I cleaned the house a little bit, watched some television, the usual." He doesn't have to know about my HGTV binge-fest. That's for me and Sir Pounce to know about. "What about you? Did you go wild? Shut down any bars? Find a girl to take home?"

The way he chuckles sends a shiver down my spine. It's a deep, guttural, dirty sound that makes me want to sit right up and say, 'Whatever you want, daddy!'

"I've told you a thousand times, Jessica," he says with that stern, fatherly tone of his, "I've only got eyes for you."

And though he blinks those brilliant green eyes at me all sweet and whatnot, I know he's just pulling my leg. Rhys is just the kind of guy who would flirt with a girl like me to make me feel better. My waist size is in the double digits, which seems a lot higher than what he's probably looking for. He's not the go big type, he'd probably rather go home.

"Maybe you should fixate those eyes on a bike." I return his stern tone with a pointed look.

The motorcycle in front of us looks like it's in a dozen pieces, but I'm sure Rhys knows what he's doing. He glances at it and then shrugs. "That?" He asks, feigning interest. "I can have that done in twenty minutes. Now *you*, on the other, that'll take longer." The wink that he gives me warms me up in more ways than one.

I can feel my cheeks flush with excitement. Sometimes when he says things like this, I wonder if I should tell him to stop. They're inappropriate comments for the workplace, but are they inappropriate when I wish he'd rip off my dress and throw me down on one of his workbenches?

Where do I draw the line?

"Hey, now," I cluck my tongue and start backing away from him. Regardless of my feelings and urges, I need to stop getting my hopes up for a guy like Rhys. "Get back to work. These people aren't paying you to feign interest in me!"

And like the scared little girl I am, I turn around and practically run to the main office to unlock the doors and greet any customers who may come in for the day.

Safe and sound, once more. From my own desires, that is.

—

"Welcome to Dirty Hands Garage, I'm Jessica." I greet a nice-looking man in a business suit as he walks through the door. "How can I help you?"

When I stand up, I notice that he takes full stock of me. I can see his pervy little eyes looking me up and down, and when his tongue slips out of his mouth to lick his lips, I can feel the vomit rise in my throat. "Sir?" I ask again, trying to speed this conversation along before I hurl. "Is there something I can help you with?"

"I came in here to grab my bike. I think it was you who called me and said it was done. I didn't realize how attractive you were on the phone though. I would have come sooner."

The only reason I know his name is because I left him a voicemail an hour ago. "Matthew, right," I nod my head in cordial recognition. "If you'd like to have a seat, I can go get Rhys to bring your motorcycle around."

"Maybe you'd like to take a ride, baby," he says when I finish speaking. "Ever been on a trike before?"

I'd rather die, thank you very much. But I think if I say that out loud, I might get fired. Or worse, I might have to apologize to him later. Neither of those sound like feasible outcomes in my book. "Let me just go get Rhys for you." I can hear the nervousness in my voice and I want to scold myself for it. This is my domain and he shouldn't make me feel this way here.

When I come out from behind the desk and head for the door leading into the mechanic's bay, I hear a low whistle and the casual 'damn' that follows it.

"The things I would do to that ass, sweetheart."

I'm not sure I hear him right, which is why I stop in my tracks. Though my cheeks flush with embarrassment and anger, I turn back to look at him with confusion. "Excuse me?" Surely a man in a suit as nice as that wouldn't come into my place of work and accost me like this. *Surely* he would know better... "What did you say?"

A guilty grin appears on his lips telling me all that I need to know. "I said I can take real good care of you, baby."

I do my best to muster a smile, holding back the vomit that wants to make an appearance if I open my mouth too wide. "I'll be right back, sir." Then I exit the door to the mechanic's bay and race to find Rhys.

When I run into him, I literally run *into* him. He's coming around a corner and I slam straight into his broad shoulders, but he manages to grab me by the elbows and steady us before we fall. "Hey there, darlin'. What's up?" When Rhys catches a glimpse of my face—probably reddened with fear and full of concern—he becomes serious. "Jessica, what's wrong?"

I don't know what to say, or how to say it, so I just point at the office while I look down at my shoes with shame.

Rhys doesn't need any other prodding. He doesn't need to know what happened, he just needs to know where to go. He pushes me aside and starts raging toward the office with me hot on his heels. "What the fuck did you do to Jessica?" He roars when he steps inside and sees the man sitting in the waiting area.

Matthew hesitates, looking between the tattooed, biker-looking dude and me and trying to determine what he should say next. "Hey, chill out, dude. I was just having some fun. I was flirting a little. I don't what she told you, but it was just a joke."

I should have gone to someone else and said something, or waited to tell Rhys until after the guy was gone. Because my boss walks right up to Matthew, pulls him out of his seat by the collar of his suit, and snarls, "Don't make me ask you again," right in his face.

"Rhys," I call his name from behind them, feeling small and embarrassed that I've caused a scene. "It's not a big deal. Just let him take his bike and leave."

"Yeah, man," Matthew stutters, "I'm not even into fat chicks anyway. I'm sorry."

Rhys pushes him away, letting him slam into the wall. "Don't you ever fucking come in here again, motherfucker. Jessica, get his keys."

I walk behind the desk, numb inside. *I'm not even into fat chicks anyway.* I grab his keys and then toss them at Rhys.

"Your shit is outside the garage. Take it and go. If I ever catch you inside here again, I'll rip your dick off and shove it so far up your ass, you'll be wearing it as a hat."

Even though Matthew takes his keys and scurries away like a scared little rodent, I'm left picking up the messy pieces of the conversation that just went down. *I'm not even into fat chicks anyway.*

"Jessica," Rhys says as he turns in my direction.

But I can't handle whatever it is he's about to say. I put my hand up to stop him and cover my mouth to keep him from seeing my lip quivering. "Give me a minute." Then I turn and walk to the bathroom, because if anyone here is going to make me cry, I'll be damned if they're going to see my tears.

Fuck Matthew. And fuck being the "fat chick" he's not into. I guess he would love my mom then.

3

RHYS

As a female, I know that Jessica is probably used to treatment like that. What Matthew said to her probably isn't even the worst she's heard, and I'm not even sure what he said to her before I arrived. But frankly, that doesn't matter. Women shouldn't be treated that way and they damn sure won't be at my shop.

Jessica is the lifeblood of Dirty Hands Garage. I know she may not realize that, but she was everything we needed to turn our dingy little shop into a full-fledged garage that people *wanted* to come to. She was the woman who did all that work. All the marketing and shit that I wasn't interested in doing? That was her. She canvased the city, put up flyers, gave out discounts, and in her first year here she doubled our profits.

I know that most of the other men don't see her as anything other than the woman who runs the business side of things, but I see her as everything I've ever imagined in my other half.

She's someone who believes in what I do and wants to see me succeed. When I hired her to run the business side, she didn't have to go above and beyond the way she did. That was just something that she did out of the goodness of her own heart, or because she genuinely believed that Dirty Hands Garage would go places. Either way, watching her help my business become one of the hottest motorcycle repair shops in the city gave me a brand new respect for her.

And even if it wasn't for that, she's gorgeous. At 5'6" and nobody cares how many pounds, she's the perfect size for me. Jessica has curves in all the right places, ones that make my dick harder than a diamond in an ice storm. She has a smile that can light up the whole room. And those blonde ringlets of hers remind me of Taylor Swift, who I only know because of my 6-year old daughter.

Don't even get me started on how good Jessica is with Danielle. Sometimes Danielle has to come to my work and wait for me when her mom's got work at the same time. Jessica prints out coloring pages for her, keeps her entertained by playing math games with her, and will even bring her around the not-so-dangerous parts of the shop to talk motorcycles with Danielle. For a girl in her early twenties, Jessica would make a great step-mom. Which is important to a guy like me.

I've spoken to some of the other guys about whether or not I should pursue something with her, but they've all been pretty tight-lipped about how they feel. I don't know if it's because one of them secretly likes her or if they just don't want to get involved with the boss' affairs, but they won't give me any advice on the matter. I actually had to ask my brother, who told me to back the fuck up before I caught a case.

"This is one of your employees? And a young one at that?" My brother did not approve. "Nah, there's other pussy out there. Run, dude, before you get yourself in trouble."

But I'm the older brother, not him. And if anyone in this family is gonna fuck up and make mistakes so that we all learn from them, it's going to be me.

—

When Jessica comes out of the bathroom, I'm sitting where Matthew was before I kicked him out. I don't want to ask her if she's okay, because that would be stupid. Obviously, she was hurt by what that idiot said and I don't want to make it worse by bringing it up and rehashing the memory.

So I just apologize for his actions instead. "If you want, I'll get you a taser to keep at the front desk," I promise her. "That way if any man, or hell, woman for all I know, ever talks to you like that again, you can tase their ass. I won't stand for you being objectified, humiliated, verbally abused, or anything like that." This woman will not be hurt on my watch.

"It's fine, Rhys," she tells me with a wan smile. "The obscene stuff he said wasn't even that crazy, it was calling me fat that got to me. I guess it shouldn't, since I am, you know, *fat*."

I take a pause to look at her, blinking as I take her all in. "What are you talking about?" I wonder if she's crazy. I wonder if she sees in the mirror the person that I see. "You're not fat, Jessica, far from it. You're beautiful. That man was just trying to cover his ass and all he did was make himself look like an ass instead."

Jessica's eyes are full of skepticism as she listens to me. It is clear that she has never heard words like this before, or if she has, it's been too long. "You don't—"

"Listen to me, you are gorgeous just the way you are. I feel like you should know that from the sheer number of times I tell you that you're beautiful, but just in case you didn't, I'm telling you again." I stand up and walk across the waiting room so that I can lean over her desk. "Jessica, you are perfect just the way you are. I don't want to change that."

"You don't want to change that?" She frowns and then stands up, mimicking my actions until her face is only inches away from my own. "Why would you even have the ability to change that? It's not like we're dating or anything. I'm just your Business Manager, Rhys. Nothing more."

She's so much more, she just doesn't realize that.

My brother's advice makes one last sprint through my mind. It's the final reminder that if I'm going to stop this before it starts, now is the time to do that.

But instead, I lean forward and press my lips against hers. She tastes of peaches. I reach up to cup her face, feeling her soft skin beneath my rough hands. Electricity shoots through my body, filling me with need and desire.

When I pull away, her eyes are closed. "I wish you'd be everything more, Jessica."

4

JESSICA

His lips pressed against mine is something I've only ever fantasized about in the dark depths of my mind where no one could tell me it was wrong, not even me.

"I wish you'd be everything more, Jessica."

And though the lingering scent of grease and arousal fills the air, I come to a full stop from his words. "Rhys, I—" I don't know what to say. He's a dominant, sexy, older man and I'm just...me. Bigger, younger, and less fun and interesting.

I've met his ex before and we look nothing alike. If I had to base his type off of her, then I'm not it. She is tall, lithe, and blonde; I'm just one of those things and I doubt blonde is the most important.

"Rhys, I don't think this is going to work out between us." It pains me to say those words, but it's true. Experience has taught me that relationships between me and men don't typically work out. When you start throwing in all the other factors between us, you get a recipe for disaster.

"I don't understand why not," Rhys' face falls, a sadness sweeping over his features that nearly breaks my heart. "What's stopping it from working out?"

He's going to make me say. All the ugly, hideous things that go through my mind when I think about us having a relationship together. "Well for starters, you're my boss." That's trouble enough by itself. "Relationships between a boss and his employee are subject to ridicule. How do we tell people that we met? We'd be a walking cliche, Rhys."

"So what?" He pushes away from the counter and crosses his arms over his chest. "What does me being your boss have to do with anything? What do people's opinions have to do with anything? If you and I were dating, we could overcome anything."

I sigh because even if that were true, that's not the only thing we have to overcome. "You're also almost twice my age, Rhys. I know people say that it doesn't matter, but it does. It can be a problem, especially when you realize that I'm not as mature as you or not in the same place emotionally." At this point, I'm beginning to think I'm in a different emotional state than him because I'm the only one who can see the flaws in this plan of ours.

"You're crazy." Rhys shrugs and walks around the desk, closing in on me. "You're older for your age than you think. You're wonderful with my daughter, with my business, and with me. You aren't every twenty-something-year-old who flies around by the seat of her pants, you're level-headed and you think things through. You are an old soul, Jessica."

I wish he'd stop making so much sense. If he could just see things through my eyes, he'd realize that he's forcing me to say these words. "Also, I'm not your type. You might think I'm fun to play around with now, but you're going to realize sooner or later that I'm a fat girl, just like that guy said earlier. I'm nothing like your ex and that's going to be a problem."

"For who?" Rhys frowns. "If I wanted a woman who was like my ex, I would have stayed with her. I want you, Jessica. That's why I'm trying to pursue you. Right here, right now. Why is that so difficult for you to see?"

"I don't know," I mumble under my breath, "I just wish I had a sign that this was right." I know that I sound silly. I can hear it. I feel like a rom-com character who's just waiting for the man to make a big romantic gesture. But just as I'm about to give up hope, he does.

Rhys steps forward and closes the distance between us, his body pressing against mine. "Maybe this will be the sign you need." And before I have the chance to question what he's doing, his lips are on mine again.

Arms snake around my waist and he pulls me impossibly closer. A flood of warmth fills my body as his tongue grazes my bottom lip, demanding entry. When I part my lips, he hungrily enters.

A hundred million, trillion voices scream at me to push him away and remind him that this can't work, that *we* can't work, but instead, I melt into his embrace.

His beard tickles my face as our tongues dance with one another. This is heaven. And I never want it to end.

5

RHYS

I reach up to run my fingers through her hair and feel my manhood pressing against my pants. "Jessica," I moan against her mouth, "I have to have you."

I want her, in more ways than one. I want to date her. I think she'd make a great lover and mother, two things I desperately want in a woman. I want to peel back the layers of her personality and see who she is when she's not at work.

She pants with desire as we break apart, her cheeks flushed. Jessica is filled with the same need that I am. "Where?" She asks, her voice on the brink of falling into ruin.

I have an office in the back. It's not very large and I rarely use it. For the last year, I've been having Jessica use it as a filing closet instead of an office, but now we're about to misappropriate it for more than folders and old records.

As I lead her down the hall and to the office, I think about all the reasons we shouldn't do this. At any point in time, this could blow up in my face. Jessica could decide I'm not the man for her. She may not enjoy the sex. She might even have a boyfriend already and she's just using me to get her rocks off. And though these thoughts hurt, I still close the office door behind us and turn the lock.

If all I have is Jessica, a dingy office, and the heat of the moment, I'm going to make the most of it.

With the door locked behind us, I turn to attack. I grab for Jessica, diving for her neck. My weakness is leaving my mark and as I lick and suck on that precious, pale skin of hers, she moans against my ministrations.

Her thick, cushy body presses against me. Jessica rubs on me like she's in heat.

I let my hands travel beneath her dress and feel her thighs. I'd love nothing more than to take this dress off of her and admire every inch of her beautiful body, but at any minute someone could walk through the front door of Dirty Hands Garage or one of my guys could come looking for me, and I don't want to waste our time.

Running my hands across the front of her silk panties, I hear a sharp intake of breath from Jessica's mouth. "Touch me, Rhys," she moans into my ear, her hands gripping my arms tightly. "I want to feel you inside of me."

I'm rockhard, but I always make sure my woman comes first. I reach inside her panties and search for her wet, hot center. Before I even touch her clit, Jessica is thrusting her hips at me. "It's been a long time since I was... last touched." There's a hint of shame in her tone.

Honestly, the less she's been touched, the better. If I ever find out who they were, I'll have a hell of a time resisting the urge to kill them if I run into them on the streets. But now that I know how much this means to her, I'll try harder.

I run my thumb across her tiny little nub and she comes alive beneath my touch. Her body shudders with desire and she slumps into me. "More, Rhys," she whispers with need.

I can *always* do more.

I start slowly circling her clit, listening to her breathing to catch a rhythm for what she's feeling. Her fingernails dig into the soft flesh of my arms. Her hips thrust toward mine, undulating in a motion that tells me she still wants more.

I increase the pace, allowing my free hand to roam all over her body and grab and feel at her voluptuous curves. She pants and moans as I bring her closer to her ecstasy. And when she tumbles over the edge of her desire, it is with her mouth firmly pressed against my shoulder to muffle her screams of pleasure.

I keep circling her clit until pulls away, that sweet little nub feeling too vulnerable and weak now that it has been wrung out of its pleasure. I hope that Jessica still wants more though, because my cock is aching to be inside of her. And not just that, I want to feel that closeness. I want to be inside of her because it would fulfill me.

6

JESSICA

Being in his forties has given him the life experience to know precisely what a woman needs to orgasm. His fingers moved in all the right ways to bring me to the height of my pleasure and then let me crash down around him.

I was terrified that someone would hear me screaming with delight when I came. So I buried my face into his shoulder and hoped that would muffle my screams. I heard a soft, smug chuckle in my ear. Rhys was proud of himself.

But this isn't over yet. I need to have him inside me. I want to feel him fucking me, taking me, *making love to me*.

"Hop up on the desk," he commands after I've had a couple of minutes to catch my breath. While I follow his orders, removing my panties as I go, he takes a few seconds to unbuckle his belt and toss it aside. "I have a condom in here somewhere," he mumbles as he searches through his wallet.

I've been with a few men over the years. Nothing crazy, but enough to know that a man who will willingly wear a condom is a rarity.

When he pulls out the foil-wrapped lifesaver, he tugs his pants down to his knees and his boxers quickly follow suit. A thick and veiny cock springs free, pointed right at me. He's the biggest I'll have ever been with.

He rips open the condom and slides it on like a professional, tossing the wrapper aside before stepping forward. "Are you ready, beautiful?"

I could say 'no'. I could end things right now and send us both back to work. But my eyes are poised on that cock and my brain is conjuring up images of fitting it inside every hole that I have. I could say 'no', but I'm not sure I could make my mouth form that word.

Instead, I spread my legs and scoot to the end of the desk. I've never been more ready for anything in my life.

Rhys places a hand on my hip to steady himself and then uses the other to guide his cock toward my entrance. Still wet from my earlier arousal, he slides right in. But it still takes me a few moments to get used to his girth, which nearly takes my breath away.

"You're so tight," he grins as he grabs my other hip with his now free hand. "You fit like a glove."

Anyone would be tight with his cock inside of them. This monster is unnatural.

I wrap my legs around his sculpted waist and draw him in, feeling him go as deep as my body can take him. The pain of new depths mixes with the pleasure of having him inside of me. I lean my forehead against his as I feel myself become used to him. "I'm ready," I breathe out after a couple of moments.

That was what he was waiting for. With my approval, Rhys slowly begins to move in and out, letting his cock massage the inside of my pussy.

What would my mother say about me finding a man now? She always said that I couldn't because I was so big, because men liked their women to be in shape. But now, as Rhys' cock pierces me over and over again and I throw my head back with pleasure, I know that's not true. There's a chance I've found a man who doesn't care about my size. He might actually like me… for me.

Rhys thrusts his monster of a member in and out of me, searching for our mutual peaks. He withdraws a hand from my hip for only a second before it lands between us, fingers desperately searching for my button. When he finds it, they furiously begin making those dangerous little circles that have already brought me to one orgasm this morning.

I can feel the sweat on both of our bodies as I pull myself into him, clawing at his back as he dives into me. The crescendo of our lovemaking meets unexpectedly and without something to muffle our sound. He roars like a lion, exploding into me as I hold onto him for dear life, doing the same. This time my orgasm is violent and almost painful.

As we come down from our high, Rhys slowly pulls out and pulls off the condom. This he doesn't discard haphazardly like the wrapper. I watch him carefully tie it off and throw it in the trash. "You know, I don't know much about you besides what I've learned here at work."

A smile is on his face as he turns back to face me. "Then you know quite a bit. I've endeavored to tell you everything. If not everything, then at least be open and honest with you."

Well, that's fair. "But I mean, I don't know your favorite color or anything."

Rhys grabs a chair and takes a seat in front of me.

We should probably go back to work, but there are some things we have to discuss. Like figuring out what comes next. A quickie in his office is one thing, but what happens when we walk out that door is something else entirely.

"What does knowing my favorite color do for you? Will knowing that it's red help you somehow?" Rhys tilts his head. "There are important little things and there are little things that are *not* important. In the beginning, you learn all those not important ones like my middle name and if I'm a morning person. But relationships thrive on the ones that you learn along the way. Like knowing that I tell the guys I take my coffee black, but secretly I load it up with hazelnut coffee creamer. Or knowing that I love French toast and making it for me after a rough week in the shop because you know it'll make my day. Those are the things I want to know about you, and the things that I hope you want to know about me. This way we can be the best possible *person* for each other."

When he puts it like that, he's right. His favorite color means nothing. But the intricate little details of our lives—the ones you find out from being around someone every day—those are everything. "Well, you know," I pull my dress down to cover my thighs, "I'll try to keep some of those little hazelnut cups here in the office then. Just in case."

His smile is back in full force his time. "That'll give me even more reason to come in and see you." I love the way his face lights up. "I love it."

I love it, too.

7

TOUCHING HER CLIENT

8

NASH

Working at a zoo has many pros and cons.

Pro: I've never had the desire to own a pet because I have hundreds at work.

Con: I still have to clean up somebody's poop and occasionally clean it off them.

But overall, the experience can't be beaten. I spend my day surrounded by elephants and lemurs, watching a new life being brought into the world, and breaking up fights.

It was making sure that Bubbles and Rose didn't tear each other apart on treat day earned me a back injury. Nothing serious, just a strained muscle that needed some TLC.

"Be sure to bring your bill to payroll," Suzie reminds me before I leave the office. "We want to make sure the zoo reimburses you for the expense."

I wave her off and shake my head. "It's not a big deal, Suz. It's just a little massage therapy. Honestly, I should have just let those two go. But Rose always bullies Bubbles and I wanted her to have a treat, too."

Suzie smiles up at me. "You're a good handler, Nash. Not everyone can take on the capuchin monkeys and live to tell the tale. You're lucky all you did was pull a muscle. We had a woman before you who had—"

I hold a hand up to stop her before she can finish that sentence. Whatever she's going to say is a horror story I don't want to mentally envision. "However this story ends, I don't need to know about it."

Suzie has stories about employees that span across three decades. I'm sure at least half of them have to do with people getting fired, injured on the job, or some combination of the two.

. . .

I play roulette with massage therapists on Google and wind up at Hansen Massage Therapy on 4th Street. Though it's a tight squeeze to find street parking, their office is quiet when I walk in.

"Nash Anderson?" The receptionist asks when I walk up to the counter. "We're going to need you to fill out some paperwork since you're a new client. Liliana is finishing up with someone right now, but she'll be with you in about ten minutes."

I expected the place to be like my chiropractor's office, complete with a skeleton of the back and soft, earthy tones. Hansen Massage Therapy has an indoor fountain, providing soothing water sounds for the waiting room. The sounds of Enya fill the rest of the void.

I sit down and begin filling out the forms the receptionist handed to me. Have I ever had a massage before? What kind of pressure do I like? Why am I here today? And a dozen other questions that probe at my level of comfort. I just want this woman to stop my muscle from throbbing in my lower back. Where's the box that I can fill out for that?

"Nash Anderson?" A sweet voice calls from across the room and my head snaps up at the sound of my name. She wears an encouraging smile on her lips as she beckons me over. "I'm Liliana. I'll be your massage therapist today. Are you finished with your paperwork?"

I feel like I'm back in middle school. My lips part slightly to respond, but no words come out. I am stricken into silence by Liliana's beauty. She swears her red locks pulled into a clip and the emerald green scrubs outline every curve of her beautiful body.

"Nash?" She frowns when I don't respond after a second. "Are you okay?"

Shit. I must look like an idiot to her. "Sorry, yes." I hand over the clipboard that the receptionist gave me and smile nonchalantly at the beautiful woman who will spend the next hour with her hands all over me. This is a dream come true, assuming my dream is PG-13. "Nice to meet you."

The smile returns as she leads me through the door and down a hallway. Her eyes scan the clipboard as she walks before flipping to the next page. When she gives a studious hum, I hope that's a good sign. I've never had a professional massage before. I wasn't sure what to write for pressure or the type of massage that I enjoyed. Maybe she can help me figure that out.

9

LILIANA

Be. Calm. Liliana. Just because your next client looks like he could be a body double for Thor doesn't mean you should lose your mind.

"This will be our room for today, Nash. You're welcome to get undressed and just knock on the door when you're ready. I'll be standing in the hall." I would rather stand here and watch him strip down, but that screams unprofessional.

I stand in the hall and do a closer inspection of his paperwork. For 'What brought you here today?' he listed 'Monkeys'. I'm not sure if he's serious or joking.

Nash knocks on the door to indicate that he's ready for me to come back in. When I do, he's standing there with a towel around his waist, showing off a six-pack of abs that nearly make me drool. "So I see on your paperwork that this is your first time."

A cheeky smile appears on Nash's lips when he says, "You can say it. I'm a virgin."

More like I could swallow my tongue. If I say those words, I'll go to hell for the thoughts that follow suit. "And I see that you listed 'monkeys' as the reason that you're here today." I look up at him with questioning in my eyes. "Want to tell me more?"

This time a blush spreads across his cheeks. "Yeah, about that," Nash reaches up to rub the back of his neck, wincing in pain at the movement. "So I was giving Bubbles and Rose their weekly treat and I wanted to make sure that Bubbles got hers this week. Rose is always trying to steal it, so I wanted to get in the middle and make sure to give each of them their treats separately. But I think Rose knew I was up to something because when I gave her a treat and didn't give one to Bubbles, she was suspicious. I waited a few minutes until she went inside and then coaxed Bubbles out to give her hers, but by then

Rose had figured out what I was doing. She came out and the next part was a blur. Anyway," he shakes his head, "long story short, I pulled a muscle in my lower back trying to keep the capuchin monkeys from tearing each other apart over a treat."

My jaw has to be dropped. That's the only thing that makes sense. Because when Nash looks up to see the horrified look on my face, he starts explaining some more.

"I'm a zoo handler. Predominantly small to medium animals, but in a pinch, I can help out with large animals as well. I'm surprised Hannah didn't do this first, frankly." Nash begins tripping over his words as if embarrassed that he started this train of thought in the first place. "She's an elephant who likes to play a little rough when she sees me. I don't know what convinced her that I'm that kind of guy. Unless she saw me fighting with—" He stops himself before he can go any further, snapping his mouth closed and laughing nervously. "Sorry about that. I'm really passionate about my job."

That's refreshing to see, honestly. I don't usually spend much time talking to my clients. I try to chat with them for the first few minutes of their session, but a lot of them are more interested in what my hands can do than making a connection with the person connected to them. "Frankly, I'm just glad I got to know the guy behind the monkey fiasco. If you hop on the table, I'll see what I can do about the muscle in your lower back."

As Nash climbs onto the massage table, I remind myself to pull it together. Even his back has muscles, rippling and bulging in just the right places. Combined with his passion for animals, he's a catch.

"Is it the lower right or lower left?"

"Right."

"Alright. I'm going to begin massaging the area. Let me know if it's too much or if you need any additional pressure." As I place my hands on his warm body, I could melt. Touching him is like touching a Greek God. He's hard in all the right places and he has muscles on muscles. I can feel the tension where he injured himself earlier today and I start there.

10

NASH

Her hands feel feather-soft, even as they knead my muscles. I could do this forever.

With my eyes closed and enjoying the sensations of Liliana's magic touch, it's not long before I fall asleep. I can still hear the sounds of Enya playing through the speakers and smell the lavender in the oil she uses to deeply massage the tissue of my back. For several minutes I drift in and out of sleep, feeling her amazing hands caress me the entire time.

When I fully come back to, I jolt upward, startled.

"Whoa there," Liliana presses a firm hand to my upper back. "Relax. You just fell asleep, Nash. Are you doing okay?"

I remember that I'm at Hansen Massage Therapy and that a beautiful, curvy woman is working the knots out of my body. Slowly I lay back down. "Yeah, I think so. I didn't realize I'd fallen asleep," I announce with sheepish embarrassment.

I can hear the smile in her voice when she says, "That's perfectly okay. People do it all the time. How is your back feeling?"

Now that she mentions it, I can no longer feel the muscle that was in pain earlier. "It feels pretty good, actually." I could probably take on the world. Or at least go another round with Rose.

Liliana removes her gentle hands from my back, leaving a cool mark where her warmth used to be. "Wonderful. If you'd like to get dressed, I'll come back in in just a moment and we can discuss if any further treatment is needed."

I watch her walk out, my eyes fixated on her round bottom, feeling every inch a creep as I watch it sway back and forth with each step.

While getting dressed I make the decision to ask her out. I know it's probably unprofessional, but Liliana is the first woman I've met in a long time that I've been genuinely attracted to. Working at the zoo has limited a lot of my interactions with the opposite gender, Rose and Bubbles excluded. I have plenty of female coworkers, but I try not to dip my pen in the company ink, so to speak.

"Are you decent?" Liliana asks before walking back into the room.

I like to think I'm a decent guy, but I know that's not what she's asking. "I'm dressed. Come on in."

Liliana hands me a couple of pieces of paper. "You should be able to practice most of these stretches at home. They'll help any residual pain you're feeling tomorrow or the day after. You're also going to want to drink plenty of water today. But otherwise, I probably won't need to see you again unless in a week or so you're still feeling pain in the muscle, in which case I'd recommend coming in again. If it's unbearable, you might see a doctor or a kinesiologist for more specialized treatment. Do you have any questions?"

"One, but it's technically not about any of this," I say, waving the papers that she gave me around. I'm sure those stretches will help and my muscle feels great, but if what she's saying is true, there's no chance that I'll see her again. My resolve to ask her out on a date is growing.

With a frown, Liliana asks, "Oh, then what is it about?"

Don't chicken out now, Nash. "I'd like to see you again, but not here. I was wondering if you might be interested in going on a date with me." *He shoots his shot...*

Her cheeks flush red and Liliana starts to stutter. "Oh, well, um, I-I-well." After a moment of this, she clears her throat and straightens up. "I would love to, actually." *...and he scores!*

"Perfect. I'd like to take you to my work this time, let you meet the culprits of what brought us together, maybe get to know a little bit more about you."

Liliana grabs her business card from a small table by the door and begins scribbling her number down on it. "I think getting to meet Rose and Bubbles would be lovely. I'll have to thank them for their hard work playing matchmaker," she says with a grin. "I get off at 5:00 if you want to call me."

I take the card from her, looking at the seven digits with a swelling heart. This day has turned around. "You can count on it, Liliana."

I walk out of the Hansen Massage Therapy office feeling on top of the world. I have a date tonight with the most beautiful girl in the world.

11

LILIANA

I don't know if you wear a summer dress to meet monkeys, but it's a warm evening and I want to wear something nice for Nash. After all, he's only seen me in my work scrubs and while that was enough to get him to ask me out, I'm hoping this turns into more.

When Nash knocks on my front door, I open it to find him wearing a loose, white, button-up shirt tucked into a pair of jeans. He wears a safari hat on his head. "Wow, you look beautiful." Nash greets with a smile.

He walks me out to his truck and helps me inside. On the way to the zoo, he tells me that he spent the rest of the day figuring out what to make for dinner and shopping for groceries. "That way, after our little zoo adventure, I can make you a nice meal. I don't cook for others often though," Nash says sheepishly. "It's usually just for myself."

That makes two of us. Most nights I make dinner for two—one plate for me to have right then, one plate for me to take for lunch the next day. On the rare occasion that I have a friend over, I don't know what to do with myself.

When we arrive at the zoo the parking lot is mostly deserted. "I have to confess that the zoo closed at 5:00, but I have keys to any exhibits we want to see. I've always thought it would be smooth to bring a woman here after hours and give her a private tour, but it just never worked out."

I feel honored that this isn't something he does regularly. There isn't a bevy of female names on a list who can say they've had this experience with Nash before. "It's very romantic. Thank you for bringing me."

Grabbing my hand, Nash leads me to a back entrance. "Rose and Bubbles are pretty shy around new people. We keep the guests behind the glass and they feel comfortable with that, but when I take you in there, we'll be on the same side of the enclosure as them."

I can't remember the last time I went to the zoo; it was probably when I was a teenager. There's some unspoken rule that when you become an adult, you leave the zoo for kids. After all, they're the ones learning what a zebra is and seeing a camel for the first time. When they wind up in the penguin exhibit or seeing a giant turtle make its way across a giant enclosure, they freak out because it's the coolest thing they've ever witnessed.

But as Nash takes me behind the veil of the zoo to see Rose and Bubbles up close, I realize that there's something I've been missing. When you're a kid, you see the zoo through fresh eyes. You see an anteater for the first time and it's exciting. But when you're an adult and you learn more about the anteater, it takes on a brand new form.

"That's Bubbles," Nash whispers, pointing toward a small capuchin monkey sitting on the highest branch of the tree. She looks down at us with suspicion in her eyes. "She's the shy one of the girls. But she loves kids. Whenever the tiny ones are hanging out in front of the window, she likes to do tricks. She'll swing from branch to branch, leaping around like she's in the circus. It makes them howl with laughter."

Slowly but surely, Bubbles comes down. At first, it's only a branch at a time. She waits on the branch, eyeing me carefully to make sure that I'm safe. Then she looks to Nash and encouragement from him makes her leap to the next branch, a few feet closer. When she's five feet away, I look at her with wonder.

"She's beautiful, Nash," I tell him breathlessly.

He smiles and squeezes my hand. "There's Rose," he points toward a gargoyle creature who hasn't moved since we entered the enclosure. She has been ten feet away the entire time, hidden in a shroud of leaves. "She'll sit by the windows whenever people come by and let them look at her, but she startles easy. There's a sign that says 'no hitting the glass' because all it takes is a knock to scare her away."

I don't know how he tells the two of them apart. I can see that there are differences, but if I turned my back on the two of the capuchins and then turned back to face them, I wouldn't know which was which. They just seem like beautiful, amazing creatures to me.

"Let's give them some privacy," Nash says after a few moments. Neither Rose nor Bubbles have moved any closer. "I think they're as comfortable as they're going to get with you at the moment. Maybe next time they'll let you pet them." He pulls me toward the exit.

Next time? That sounds encouraging. I let Nash lead me out of the enclosure, feeling closer to him than when I had my hands all over him earlier today.

12

NASH

I saw the way her face lit up when Bubbles got closer. I hated to take Liliana out of the enclosure, but I didn't want to risk either of the capuchins getting aggressive and attacking. With her red tresses water falling down her back, they would have gripped onto those and never let go.

"Thank you for bringing me here, Nash," she exclaims when the door to the enclosure is closed behind us. "This was an amazing experience. I feel..." Liliana trails off, looking for the right word.

I smile at her and shrug. "You don't have to thank me. It's a beautiful place. Being here, behind the scenes, is something else. I learn something new about the animals every day. They each have their own personalities and getting them to trust you and open up to you is such a rewarding experience."

Liliana comes in closer to me, pressing her lips against my cheek. "Your passion for what you do is inspiring. I love that you are dedicated to these animals."

I turn my head just a fraction to make eye contact with her, looking into her beautiful, brown eyes. "I'm dedicated to everything in my life. Maybe the next thing I can be dedicated to... is you."

A tinge of pink comes to her cheeks and she looks down between the two of us. "Nash, I have to be honest with you. I don't understand why you're attracted to me."

The shame in her voice sets me on fire. Could it be that this woman doesn't realize how beautiful she is? I grab her chin and tilt her head up until her eyes are looking into mine again. "Hey now, I think you're gorgeous. You also let me rant in your massage room about my monkeys without judgment. I think that's an excellent quality to have when half of my day is dealing with a variety of small animals who think throwing stuff at me is a game."

When a smile curves around her lips and a giggle bubbles from her lips, I'm smitten. "And I'm not kidding *at all* about the gorgeous part. You came out to get me in those skin-tight scrubs and I had to remind myself that I was out in public. I had half a dozen dirty thoughts before I even crossed the room to come say hello."

Liliana bites her lip and looks down again. "Nash," the way she says my name is enchanting, "you barely know me."

"But I knew right then that I wanted you. And I'm not a one-night stand kind of guy. You walked out so I could get dressed and I was considering all the ways I could convince you to go out with me." Not to mention all the ways I could talk her out of her clothes. I wanted to feel her curves. I needed to grab her ass. I wanted those thighs wrapped around me as she rode my face.

"Have you ever," Liliana pauses and then looks up at me between her long, thick eyelashes, "had sex here at the zoo?"

My dick is as hard as a diamond in an ice storm. "No, but I've always wanted to." I hope she doesn't hear the desperation in my voice.

"And where have you always wanted to have sex?" She asks with a touch of naughtiness to her tone. Her tongue comes out, licking her bottom lip.

I nearly have to pinch myself to make sure I'm awake. This can't be happening. "The polar bear exhibit," I say without hesitation.

Liliana squeezes my hand in hers and looks around. "Well then, lead the way, Nash."

Good Lord. This is really happening.

My heart is racing as I lead Liliana through the exit and start making my way toward the polar bear exhibit. They have a large pool that can be viewed from an underground seating area. In the evening, when the sun is going down, the water casts a beautiful, illuminating glow. I can't wait to see Liliana basking in it.

13

LILIANA

I don't know what came over me. It was probably the fact that I haven't had sex in a while. And by 'while' I mean almost a year. He wasn't even that good, either. He didn't care about my needs, he didn't make me orgasm, and in the end, he got up and walked out without so much as a 'thank you'.

But I know that Nash isn't that type of guy. Someone who cares about animals as much as Nash does could never be a *wham, bam, thank you, ma'am* kind of guy.

When he leads me down the stairs and into the polar bear exhibit, I come face-to-face with the interior of their pool. I see polar bears swimming, looking at us the way we're looking at them. Above the water is another polar bear standing on some rocks and looking pensive.

Before I have a chance to get immersed in the beauty of the exhibit, Nash pulls me into his hard chest and his lips crash upon mine with urgency. Just this morning I was thinking about what a hard-bodied, hot piece of ass he was. Now here he is, hands snaking around my waist to pull me as close as he can get me.

It's all I can do to stop myself from moaning when his fingers travel up my spine and get lost in my hair, twirling the locks and gently tugging at the strands.

I can feel his cock pressing against the zipper of his jeans, desperately trying to make a bid for freedom. I drop a hand between the two of us and graze over the bulge, feeling how hard he is beneath the fabric.

"Fuck," he whispers vulgarly into my mouth, "Is this really happening?"

I fumble with his belt, making my intentions obvious. "Only if you want it to, Nash," I whisper hungrily, hoping to God that he wants this as much as I do.

He hesitates for a moment and I question if I'm going too fast for him. Should I slow down? Should I save this for another day? After all, we did just meet.

But before I have a chance to overthink this moment any further, he leads me over to the seating area and sits me down on the bench. "Let me show you how much I want to, Liliana." The hunger in his eyes makes me clench my thighs with desire. "Take off your panties," he says as he drops to his knees in front of me.

I stand up for just a moment and reach beneath my dress to pull down the lacy white thong I wore tonight to make me feel confident. I guess it worked because here I am, about to get eaten out while watching the polar bears. The thought of his tongue licking me to orgasm sends a shiver down my spine.

I sit back down on the edge of the bench and pull up the skirt of my dress, unveiling my bald pussy for his waiting eyes.

"A pre-dinner appetizer," he says with a grin as he parts my legs even more. "Looks tasty." He begins to kiss his way from my knee, down my thigh, and right to that sensitive little spot that sends electrical shocks through my body. While he's working on my swollen clit, two fingers find my slick entrance and make their way inside. His other hand moves upward, grabbing onto my waist for support.

I grab onto the bench to hold myself steady as his teeth graze over my clit. They send me toward the edge of my desire before bringing me back down with the slow, languorous lick of his tongue. His fingers curl toward my G-spot, pumping in and out as he tantalizes that sweet little nub from the inside.

A thin layer of sweat breaks out across my brow as I throw my head back, taking in all the sensations from his fingers and his mouth. When he closes his lips around my swollen bud and begins to gently suck while flicking his tongue, I press against his face as my climax comes to a head.

Nash is careful to keep the stimulation going, ensuring that I ride the wave of my orgasm until it's over. As he feels me pull away from his ministrations, he slowly withdraws his fingers pulls his head out from beneath my dress.

I see my arousal on his lips and I blush with embarrassment. "I'm sorry," I say with a nervous chuckle.

"Don't be," he shrugs before thoroughly licking his lips. "That was exactly what I wanted. You taste sweet and delicious."

No man has ever said that to me before, but no man has ever made me come like that before, either. My need for him increases. "Get on the bench," I instruct, "I want to get on top of you."

Nash grins like today's his lucky day. He gets on his feet and works to remove his belt and pull down his jeans, letting his cock spring free.

I knew he was decently proportioned just by feeling his hardness pressed against me, but seeing it in this capacity is breathtaking. Dick pics are never pretty, but his thick, veiny cock pointing right at me as he makes himself comfortable on the bench is a thing of beauty.

14

NASH

I lean back against the second bench and make room for Liliana on my lap. She climbs on top and immediately dives for my neck, her lips roaming across the skin, kissing and sucking as her fingers skillfully unbutton my shirt.

"When I saw your body earlier at my office, I wanted to touch every inch of it," Liliana whispers into my ear. When the last button is freed, she reaches inside and begins running her hands across my abs, feeling me up.

I take this time to grab her ass beneath her dress, feeling the thick, luscious bottom that I fantasized about earlier in the day. "I can't wait to be inside of you," I moan into her ear.

If that was a challenge, Liliana rises to the occasion. She reaches between her thighs and grabs my cock with one of her hands, leading it to her entrance. "The wait is over," she says with a chuckle.

Lowering herself onto my cock, I can barely restrain myself. Her pussy envelopes my member, tightening around me as she breathes out low and slow.

"Oh, fuck." The swear slips out when she comes to a rest on my lap, my cock as far inside of her as it will go. It'll be a miracle if I don't blow my load after two pumps.

Liliana lifts her hips and then drops back onto my cock. Her breasts bounce right in my face, driving me wild. When she rises up again, I thrust my hips up to meet her on the way down. When I run a hand between her legs to massage her clit as she rides my cock, she has to grab onto the second bench to keep herself steady as she undulates her hips.

I can tell she's on her way toward her peak when her movements change. She becomes more erratic, lifting her hips and falling with less rhythm and more speed. And when orgasms for the second time, her breasts arch into my face as she takes her pleasure with greed.

I follow with her name on my lips, hoping to God that there's nobody around. Night staff should be arriving soon, but I pray they won't arrive while Liliana is on my lap with my juices dripping out of her.

Hand-in-hand we lazily walk through the zoo. A smile is plastered on Liliana's face, one that I'm sure is mirrored on my own.

"I don't usually do this, you know," she says as we pass the elephants.

I glance over at her in the setting sun and raise an eyebrow. She looks beautiful, especially knowing what we've just done together. "Do what?"

Liliana's smile grows. "You know, have sex with men who are relative strangers. This is a new one for me. I don't have sex on the first date and *definitely* not before he's made me dinner."

It occurs to me that I would make her more than dinner if she asked. Tonight has been an amazing experience for me, and not just because I got to cross something off my sex bucket list. "If it makes you feel any better, I'm still going to make you dinner. I'm even going to call you again tomorrow. I may even send you an up-close and personal photo of Bubbles, if she's feeling photogenic."

"I won't send you pictures of any of my clients," Liliana promises me quickly. "For starters, that would be a privacy violation. But also, my clients are quite as cute as yours."

I think I'm half in love with this woman already. I don't know why. Maybe it was watching the sheer joy on her face when meeting the capuchins for the first time, or watching that same look return when I gave her an orgasm. Knowing that she received delight from what I did—professionally and sexually—stirs something inside of me that I can't explain. "If it's okay with you, I'd like to take you back to my place now."

Liliana's eyes grow larger and she looks around. "Nash," she admonishes quietly since a night employee is walking by.

"What?" I ask innocently. "I want to make you dinner. If you recall, we still haven't eaten. Well," I grin, "I have, but you might still be hungry."

Her cheeks blush red and she smacks my arm lightly. "You're horrible, Nash Anderson."

"I'll be anything for you, Liliana."

15

ONE NIGHT WITH HER BOSS

16

JAXON

The line outside 295 wraps around the building. Men wear their best dancing clothes and women don their shortest dresses. Everyone wants into 295.

It's been two months since the doors of the bar opened. When I bought this building almost a year ago, it seemed like a pipe dream. I wanted to create the hippest, trendiest bar on the west side of town. My friends laughed at me and my dad seemed skeptical, but he still gave me the funds to get started. But now people filter in to get a handmade cocktail, enjoy a couple of hours on the dance floor, and maybe find the perfect person to take home at the end of the night.

I'm a nightclub cupid, shooting men and women across the county with my arrows made of top-shelf vodka.

"Jax, we're out of vodka."

Shit. That's the second night in a row this has happened. I need to increase our supply because the demand is hurting my pocketbook. "I'll run to the liquor store!"

It's only 11:30. If I don't grab another case of vodka to make it to 2:00 am when the bar closes down, I'll have a riot on my hands.

I head out of the backdoor of 295 and get into my car. Working from 6:00 pm - 4:00 am every day is exhausting, but I doubt I'd ever change it. Opening my own bar has been my dream ever since I turned 21; I'm not about to give that up for a regular 9—5 work schedule.

The liquor store closes at midnight and the woman working is sweeping up when I arrive. Her red locks are piled in a clip on the top of her head. Escaped tendrils drip down and frame her face. Either it's late or this woman is kind of beautiful.

"Good evening, sir," she greets me with a pleasant smile when I walk through the doors. "We're closing up here in a few minutes. Is there something I can help you find?"

She oozes sexuality. Her shirt dips low enough that I see the curve of her breast. Her pants hug her round, ample bottom. "Are you looking for a job?"

She doesn't seem put off by the strange, out-of-left-field comment; she only raises an eyebrow and leans against the broom she was using the sweep. "You mean besides this one?" She nods toward the cash register just a few feet away. "Listen, sir, I don't know what you're pushing, but I'm not—"

I put my hands up to stop her. I know what I must look like. A guy wearing black pants and a button-down shirt that's unbuttoned halfway down my chest. I'm sure I give off the impression of being a sleazeball. "I'm Jaxon Ellington and I own 295 down the road. I don't mean to be disrespectful at all, but I think I could use you."

A giggle slips through those plump lips of hers. "Use me, huh?" She returns to her job sweeping up the floors, shaking her head as she goes.

Now that she mentions it, I did use some pretty unfortunate language to describe the role I envisioned for her. "I didn't mean it like that." I lean up against the counter and watch her work. She moves with the confidence of a woman who doesn't give a shit what I think about her. Half the women at 295 could stand to learn a thing or two from her. "What's your name?"

She stops sweeping again, this time to let out a huff. "My name is Kate and like I said, I'm not interested. If you don't mind getting what you came here for and checking out, I'd like to close down soon."

She isn't too rough around the edges, just matter-of-fact. "How do you handle drunk people?"

"What is this, some kind of informal interview?" Kate pushes a strand of hair out of her face and stands up straight. "I've got a perfectly good job here and—"

She doesn't know what she's turning down and I can prove it. "I'll make you the shot girl. Guaranteed $5 an hour. You take home any tips you make. For every $100 you sell, you get a $10 bonus. The shot girls have been walking out with over $150 in tips a night, plus what they make in hourly and from the bonus. Usually, you work from about 9:00 pm to 3:00 am. Let's say you make about $200 from everything. That boils down to just over $30 an hour. Still not interested?"

I don't know Kate personally, but it looks like she's struggling internally with what to say. Her eyebrows knit together and I can practically see numbers whizzing past the forefront of her brain. "You've got the look, you know," I tell her after a couple moments of silence.

"What look?" Kate's tone is sharp and reeks of offense.

As a woman with a curvy body, I can see how she might take what I said the wrong way. "Don't get me twisted, you're gorgeous. But you have this way about you. When you move, it's intoxicating to watch. I think you'll do well at 295."

Kate purses her lips and stares at me for a fraction of a second before turning on her heel and going behind the liquor counter. She starts rummaging through a drawer before pulling out a card and handing it to me.

Kate Ludlow Assistant Manager of Lucky Strike Liquor 407-555-8422

"That's my cell number," she explains as I look over the card. "I'm free on Thursday and Saturday nights."

I really need a girl who will work Fridays, too, but I'll take what I can get. "Thank you, Miss Ludlow." I pull out my wallet and slip her card inside, exchanging it for my own. "Tomorrow afternoon I want you to call me. I want to show you around 295 so you can get a feel for the place and see if you like it."

Without looking at my card, Kate shoves it into the back pocket of her jeans. "I wasn't kidding about closing soon though. Get whatever you're here for before I have to cut you off. I don't stay open late for anyone." Her attitude says she doesn't give a shit if I just offered her a job; she wants to go home and I'm not going to be the asshole that stops that from happening.

I tip an imaginary hat at Kate. "Wouldn't dream of keeping you up past your bedtime, sweetheart. I need a case of vodka though."

The nickname irks her; I can see the annoyance on her face. Kate rolls her eyes and heads to the back to grab what I need. "I appreciate your help tonight," I say graciously when she's checking me out. "I probably wasted too much time here talking to you, but I think it'll be worth it in the long run. You've got something special about you, Kate."

A tiny pink tongue pops out of her mouth and licks her bottom lip. "Yeah, yeah, whatever. I'm only checking it out to see if you're right about that $30 an hour thing."

Damn. The women at 295 are practically falling on me from the minute we open the doors until closing time. But Kate couldn't give two shits about who I am or what I look like. "So you're not coming because I'm charming and good-looking?"

With an unladylike snort, she hands my card back to me. "You wish, honey. You're not really my type."

That's the first time a woman has ever said that to me. I'm every woman's type. I'm tall, tanned, and have a body fat percentage in the single digits. "And what's your type?" I have to know.

"The kind who won't break like a twig when I sit on their face."

I'm appalled by the suggestion that I wouldn't be able to handle her thick thighs wrapped around my head. That's how I've always wanted to go out and if the Lord saw fit for me to be smothered to death by a curvy girl, so be it. "Call me tomorrow, gorgeous."

"Call me Kate. I don't do pet names."

Have mercy. Is this what love feels like? Because I'm half terrified she might punch me if I say the wrong thing, but the other half of me wants to strip her down and let her ride me like a carnival horse.

17

KATE

A quick Google search tells me that 295 is the hottest new club in town. Opened by the young and devilishly handsome Jaxon Ellington, there isn't a single word of bad press on the internet. Further digging tells me Jaxon is a cool thirty-one years old. His father is big in the tech industry and has more money than God.

If I was the gold-digging type, I'd take him up on his flirtatious banter. Instead, I give him the requested call and find out what I need to do to start working.

When he started throwing out numbers, I'll have to admit that I was more than enticed by the idea of working for him. $150 in tips for six hours of work is worth it even without the hourly pay and sales bonuses. The possibility of walking out the door with over $200 twice a week? It sounded like a steal.

I'm not a proud woman. I know when I'm bested in a fight. Which was why he reeled me in so quickly after throwing out how much I could make. I've got bills to pay and a mortgage that doesn't wait until I'm in a good financial place to request to be paid.

"Wear something tight and show up with your I-don't-give-a-fuck attitude and you'll knock them dead," Jaxon said over the phone.

I bet he didn't expect a bustier coming. To be honest, I didn't either. But I called a girlfriend and asked her what the best thing to wear as a shot girl was and she said it didn't matter, as long as there was cleavage showing. Your tits don't pop out any further than when you're wearing something that cinches you up and shows off the girls.

I walk into 295 with my head held high and my party pony even higher. I can hear the laughter of the other girls as they get ready for the night, but I beeline straight for the bartender. "Hey. Is Jaxon Ellington around?"

The bartender looks like he missed out on his emo phase in high school and he's trying to recreate it ten years later. He probably wouldn't look so bad if it wasn't for the overdone eyeliner. "That depends. What are you here for?"

He's gatekeeping for the boss. How cute. "I'm from the Alcoholic Beverage Control Board and I've been given orders to remove Mr. Ellington's liquor license." Too bad he's not as cute when his eyes are bugging out of his head and he thinks he's about to lose his job.

"I'll uh, I'll get Jaxon. He's upstairs." He makes his way to the spiral staircase that leads to the second floor, shuffling his feet and almost wiping sweat off his brow.

It takes less than a minute for Jaxon to poke his head around the corner with a concerned look on his face and the poor bartender hot on his heels. When he peers over the railing and sees me standing by the bar, he lets out a laugh that can be heard throughout the building.

Jaxon and the bartender descend the staircase looking like two sides of a coin. Jaxon wears a smile on his face and the bartender looks angry and hurt.

"You're with the Alcoholic Beverage Control Board?" Jaxon asks with a condescending tone when he reaches me.

I give him a shrug and throw an apathetic apology at the bartender. "It came to me in the moment."

"You nearly gave Scott a heart attack. He busted into my office looking like he'd seen a ghost."

Scott walked around the bar mumbling under his breath. I swear I heard the word 'bitch' come out of his mouth, but oh well. "Did you consider possibly telling anyone that I was coming so I didn't walk in here with absolutely no idea where to go or who to speak to?"

A smirk crosses his face and he looks positively amused with himself. "You found me, didn't you?"

"Through a great deal of pain and suffering. Sure." I'm beginning to dislike this man. He may have offered me the job of a lifetime paying more in a day than my current hourly wage, but that doesn't mean that I like him.

"Well I have to say, you look good, gorgeous. The men here are going to eat you up." Jaxon looks me up and down, taking in every inch of me with those honey-brown eyes of his. They make you want to melt until they're lit on fire with lust. Then the twinkling makes you vaguely aware that this man is interested in far more than what I can do for his sales.

That's fine. I've dealt with men who say more with their big mouths than Jaxon says with his eyes. I can handle being a little eye candy for the boss in exchange for $30+ an hour. "Hey, buddy. Eyes up here," I point toward my face. "If you want to look, it's going to cost."

I said the wrong thing. Jaxon's eyebrow shoots up into his hairline and his lips curl into a smile. "Oh, yeah?" He pulls his wallet out of his back pocket and opens it up. "Give me a number, sweetheart. I'm happy to pay if it means I get to look all night."

Despite myself, I smile. He's smooth. He's handsome. Most of all, he knows how to take a joke. A man with a sense of humor is attractive. "Okay, playboy, what's the deal here? What am I supposed to be doing?"

"Down to business. Got it." He nods his head in mock agreement. "We'll come back to this later." The way Jaxon says 'this' and winks at me sends a shiver down my spine. "So it's pretty simple. Tonight you'll carry around a tray of shots. Your job is to sell them quickly and come back to the bar for another round. Think you can do that?"

I snort at him in a very unladylike fashion. "Honey, I sell alcohol for a living. This is basically an extension of my current job, but with tighter fitting clothing."

Jaxon's grin makes my knees weak. "We'll provide you with a fanny pack to collect cash for the shots. Any questions, gorgeous?"

"Only one." I look around at the other girls who are eyeing us with looks of jealousy. "Do you flirt with the other girls like this or am I getting special treatment?" I'm not here to get in catfights with the other ladies. I just want to make my money and leave.

"What other girls?" Jaxon asks, oblivious for a split second before he looks around and sees nearly a dozen of them milling about. "Oh, them. Nope. I only have eyes for you."

Great. A sexy man whose attention has fallen on the new girl is definitely going to earn me some new friends. I can see it now.

18

JAXON

It is an absolute joy to watch Kate work. She moves through the crowd like she's royalty, not needing to shove or push people out of her way. Usually, the shot girls struggle to make it through big groups, but Kate slips through like butter. Not to mention people are buying shots from her at an astounding rate.

In the first hour, I watch her make two trips back to the bar. I do the math in my head. If she has twenty shots on the tray and each of them is selling for $3 apiece, by the time she's finished with her third tray she's made me a cool $180 and it's barely 11 pm. The other two shot girls on deck for tonight are finishing up their first tray, which is on par for them.

I think in some sick way, people are less and more terrified of Kate than the other girls. She doesn't remind them of a long, lithe model with perfect bouncy hair and a flat stomach, so she's less threatening. Women feel like they can buy from her because she's relatable and men buy because they think they have a chance.

But at the same time, she's gorgeous in her own right. With her tits on display and that blindingly beautiful smile of hers, she catches people off guard. They support her with their cash in the form of tips and purchases. She is utterly disarming, which is precisely what I need.

Hiring Kate has been more than just a strategic business move. I had some time to think and reflect about it after I went home and I'm pretty sure in the heat of the moment, my dick was part of the decision-making process. I didn't know it at the time, but it makes sense. I'm not the kind of business owner who hands out jobs like they're candy. I try to give jobs to people I believe will do good in their roles. I didn't even interview Kate; I just offered her a position based on how she made me feel.

Kate reeks of confidence. Women her size with their thick hips you can grab onto and chests that you can bury your face into often don't have that kind of confidence in themselves. And I've never understood why. They are big, beautiful women that you can sink your teeth into. I'm the kind of guy who wants a woman like that. And considering the men who stare at her longingly, Kate is more than a few guys' type.

I watch her make her way through the crowd like Moses parting the sea. People move aside for her and watch in awe, just like me. I find myself traveling from group to group to check in and see how people are enjoying 295. Then, before I can stop myself, my eyes start searching for her. I see her standing in the middle of a group of men, taking their cash and laughing so naturally that she could be part of their circle. Kate fits in, she knows how to insert herself into a conversation with ease and leave just as transparently.

Kate has a way about her that's impossibly intoxicating. I know nothing about her, but I want to know more.

19

KATE

The gig is easy. Selling is about playing to a person's wants and desires and learning how to handle rejection. Not everyone can do it, but it's been my entire career.

At 1:45 in the wee hours of the morning, the bartenders call last call. There's a mad rush to the bar to grab drinks, but I just hang out a few feet away from the bar and offer shots to anyone who won't make it to the front of the line. Some drunk people snub me while others buy shots, knowing their last chance for drunkenness depends on a quick 40% alcohol content to the head.

By the time the place closes at 2:00 and the security guards have pushed everyone out, my feet ache and my body hurts. It's been a long night slinging shots and I'm sure I'll be exhausted in the morning.

"You did good, kid," Jaxon says as I sidle up to the bar with my fanny pack full of money. "I was watching you throughout the night to see how you'd do."

I roll my eyes at him, but I can't stop the smile forming on my lips. "I bet that's not the only reason you were watching me," I tease. I know I sold north of $400 worth of shots. That extra $40 in sales incentives is like a shot of its own, sending me straight to the moon.

Jaxon throws his hands up in defense and shrugs. "Hey, I'll pay out whatever you want for watching you tonight, sweetheart. You worked that floor like you'd been doing it all your life. I'd like to see you out here again whenever possible."

I don't know how often that'll be. On Thursdays and Saturdays, I'm the opener at the liquor store, that's why I was okay with working at 295 for the night. On Fridays I'm the woman who closes up shop; it's why Jaxon found me sweeping up when he came in last night. "We'll see, boss. I've got a lot going on in my life. Thursdays and Saturdays might be the only days you can have me."

That was the wrong choice of words. "I'll take you anytime, baby. Just say the word."

It feels odd to have a man like Jaxon practically drooling over me. In one aspect, it makes me uncomfortable because it's not something that's ever happened to me before. I can pick up men, but I never pick up men who look like him. In another aspect, it gives me the confidence to shoot him a wink and stick out my tongue at him in a slightly juvenile manner. Nothing makes a girl feel good in her skin like having a rich man with muscle definition look at you like you're a steak he can't wait to devour.

"I feel like you're trouble," I announce with a shrug as I hand my cash over to the bartender.

Scott will do the work tallying up how much I owe 295 for the shots I checked out tonight and whatever's left is my tip out for the night. I'm pretty confident it's in the three-figure range.

"I'm whatever you want me to be, beautiful."

I just want him to be himself. This smooth-talking son of a bitch who knows the right words to put me on the edge of my seat is bad news. I don't need a walking, talking sex god in my presence; that'll make me act up.

Scott, who's been ignoring our banter this whole time, slides a pile of money over the bar to me. "The rest is yours, Kate." The cold tone in his voice tells me that he's still not over my little joke earlier about yanking 295's liquor license. Poor kid.

I take the time to arrange and count my money. I've never wanted to be a stripper, but I sure feel like one as I count out $56 in one-dollar bills. With $50 in 5s, $30 in 10s, and $60 in 20s, I feel like I'm on top of the world. That's $196 in tips, plus $40 in sales incentives. "It was a pleasure working here tonight," I grin up at Jaxon as I shove the wad of cash into my bra. I didn't wear clothes with pockets, so this is all I've got to work with.

"If you need any more pleasure, please let me know. I'm always available."

This man just doesn't quit. When he sees something he wants, he really goes for it. And maybe it's the money-high or the confidence from being showered with attention from a male specimen who is truly a better class than some of the men I've fucked with, but I'm going to go for it. What do I have to lose besides a little pride? It's not like Jaxon strikes me as the kind of guy who's interested in a relationship. A little physical release wouldn't hurt anyone, right?

"Always available, huh?" I look around to make sure that none of the other women are around. The bartenders are cleaning up and Scott is counting cash for one of the other shot girls. If I'm going to make my move, now's the chance. "You think you can handle a girl like me?"

Jaxon's eyes light up like it's Christmas and I'm the present waiting under the tree for him. "Gorgeous, I can handle you over and over again, all night long. Just say the word and we can blow this popsicle stand."

It's poor form to have sex with your boss. It's probably even frowned upon in most businesses. But most bosses don't look like Jaxon Ellington, and that's a game-changer for me. "How about a quickie in the parking lot?" I ask with a raised eyebrow and a shrug. "It's pretty late, you know. I've got stuff to do in the morning."

"Help finish cleaning up with the rest of the girls and I'll see you in the back lot in twenty minutes."

Oh, honey. I'm going to rock your world in twenty minutes.

20

JAXON

There's a chance this gorgeous young woman is fucking with me, but it's a chance I'm going to take.

I rush the others to finish cleaning up quicker. I want them out of here. They don't have to go home, but they can't stay here.

While they finish the clean-up work, I head out to my car to make sure everything is sorted. I don't want Kate feeling uncomfortable surrounded by paperwork. I throw everything in the front seat except for the blanket I keep in the back for emergencies. I spread that out over the seat and try to make a comfortable bed for me and my soon-to-be lover.

I'm not stupid. I know Kate isn't interested in me as a person. Why would she be? She doesn't know my middle name, she's never met my friends, and she has no idea who I am outside of running 295. I can accept that I'm strictly a piece of meat to this gorgeous broad, but I'd like to see if she's just as fascinating when she's not on the clock. Is she always this biting and acerbic? Or does she have layers?

I see her step out of the backdoor of 295 with the rest of the staff. Scott locks the door behind everyone and they all disperse to their cars. It's nearing 3 am and most of them look dead tired, but there's a naughty twinkle in Kate's eye that tells me she's still ready for some fun tonight.

"Tidying up?" She asks as she walks over.

"Wouldn't want you to kneel on important paperwork, like my taxes or the employee handbook."

Kate grabs the handle of my car door and opens it. "Oh, no. Not the employee handbook. Not the only document telling us that we shouldn't do this."

I smack her ass as she climbs in the backseat of my car. "You're too damn sassy for your own good."

A little squeal emits from her lips at the smack. Her head flickers back in my direction and she narrows her eyes at me. "When I asked if you could handle me, I meant all of me. Sass included."

That sounds like a threat. But I don't cave to pressure easily. "Make some room, gorgeous. Trust me, you could ride me all night and I'd still be asking for more." If given the chance, I'll make use of her sassy mouth in other ways. Maybe not tonight, but maybe in the future.

Kate doesn't take her time. When she has herself situated on one end of the car, she starts grabbing the waistband of her tight, black pants and pulls them down.

"Whoa there, sugar. I thought I was going to do that for you." I don't want this to go too fast; I want to enjoy her.

She only rolls her eyes at me. "Maybe if we were in a proper bedroom, I'd give you the chance to take off my pants. But out here?" Kate shakes her head 'no'. "You can spend more time figuring out how to make me orgasm instead. No orgasm, no second secret affair."

So she might be interested in doing this again? By all means, I'll gladly partake. It would be easier to get her off with my tongue and a couple of fingers, but if all I've got is limited space and the opportunity to bury my face in her chest, I'll make it work.

21

KATE

Jaxon's a talker. He has been in every situation I've encountered him in so far. But now that I'm sitting before him in just a bustier and panties, he's at a loss for words.

"Just take me, Jaxon, before I change my mind." The impatience is real. I could already be halfway to getting off if I went home to my vibrator.

He doesn't need any further encouragement before he slides across the seat and buries his face in my neck. One hand works at my bustier, trying to find a way beneath the material to pull one of my breasts out. When it's finally free, Jaxon redirects his attention to the erect nipple.

First, his fingers pull at the tiny pink bud, then his mouth is on top of it, swirling hot and wet circles with his tongue. I lean against the door and let the pleasurable sensations wash over me.

The last man I was with didn't want to see me fully naked. But Jaxon can't seem to get enough of me. He's tugging at my panties and whispering into my chest that he wishes I'd take the bustier off. It would probably be more comfortable if I did, but I'll never get that cinched back up in the backseat of his car.

Jaxon navigates the curves and contortions of my body to remove the last vestiges of my privacy. I sit before him with just my stomach and part of my breasts hidden. In any other universe I'd feel self-conscious, but being with Jaxon gives me confidence.

With my body unveiled before him, Jaxon makes quick work of his own pants. They come down just far enough to expose his cock. In the glint of the moonlight, I can already see the precum leaking from his tip.

"Oh, shit," he swears as he leans over the center console to push through some papers upfront. "Got it!" Jaxon announces after a second and then comes back to the backseat. In his hands in a foil-wrapped condom, perfect for protecting us in this sensitive moment. "You still ready for this?" He asks as he rips open the condom and starts to roll it down his cock.

I appreciate him asking and making sure he still has my consent. But now that I've seen his thick, veiny member, I wouldn't back out if you paid me. I want to have that monster inside of me, swollen and pulsating along with my own body. "Ready and willing." And maybe a little more.

He grabs me by the legs and pulls me further down in the seat until I'm on my back. "I want you to be comfortable." Then just as quickly, Jaxon's lips are on mine. For the first time since I met him, we share a kiss. He's soft and tastes of whiskey.

Against my thigh, I feel his engorged member. He's even bigger when he's pressed against me. "Put it in," I whisper into his ear, desperate to feel him inside me and moving around. It's late and I'm tired of waiting for my release.

I reach between my legs and grab, and Jaxon moans at my touch. I guide his thick cock to my entrance; it is slick with my desire. As he slowly enters his tip, a feeling of relief washes over me. It's like breaking the seal on a jar of pickles; it's satisfying.

I kick my leg up on one of his seats to allow for deeper penetration and Jaxon is happy to oblige. He buries himself in me, his cock filling me up. "Fuck, you feel so good," he groans when he's all the way inside.

I wish this moment would last forever. This man's hard body is pressed against mine, his cock is deep inside me, and even though the car isn't the most comfortable location to be doing this, it feels right.

Jaxon starts to move, slowly undulating his hips in and out of me. I grab onto his bicep and dig in with my nails with one hand while the other travels back between my legs. I reach for my clit, fingering the hard nub as Jaxon massages my insides with his cock.

"God, even with this condom on, you make me want to explode." He swears as he starts thrusting faster.

There's a dull thrumming in my clit as I make furious circles around it. The electricity of his cock inside me sends waves straight to my pleasure zone.

"Fuck me harder," I demand, desperate to reach for my aching desire.

Jaxon is nothing if not cooperative. I let go of his bicep and grab his ass to feel it flex every time he enters me. He moves like a skilled surgeon, using his cock to find just the right places to send me straight to the moon.

I am shocked when our pleasure reaches its peak at the same time. I wrap my legs around his waist to pull him closer, releasing a yell that can probably be heard all the way to the next block. Jaxon lets out a lion's roar of desire, emptying himself while still pumping.

This man is a different breed. I've never met anyone like him before. Humorous, able to put up with my sass, and very interested in me.

His sweaty forehead lays against mine when his orgasm is complete. "Do you believe in love at first sight? Because I think you're the girl of my dreams."

Despite the post-orgasmic confession, I have to laugh at him. "This is hardly love at first sight. You met me yesterday."

"And I thought there was something different and beautiful about you then, too."

I swallow back the lump forming in my throat. He's not like the men I've dated before. He loves a confident woman, and that's who I am. And he loves a curvy woman, which is also who I am. "Yeah, yeah," I say, attempting to affect my sarcastic tone from earlier in the night, "this doesn't mean anything though." I don't want to get hurt. I hope he realizes that.

"Of course not," Jaxon says with a grin, pressing his lips against mine for a second kiss. "Do you want to not mean anything to each other later this week? Maybe we can grab dinner first. Then I'll not mean anything to you in a proper bed where you can sit on my face and I can make you scream my name."

I don't believe in love at first sight, but I do believe in chance encounters. He might just be the perfect man for me, and if it wasn't for 295 running out of vodka last night, I might never have met him. "I like sushi."

"And I like you."

I'm probably asking for trouble by sleeping with the boss, but it's the best-looking trouble I've ever been in. This handsome man could break me, yet somehow I don't think he will. And that makes all the difference.

22

CHARMED BY HER BOSS

23

IVY

The job description was for one of New York's busiest, most focused financial investors, but as I look around the room and see 5'10" models wearing stilettos and short skirts, I wonder if I missed some kind of subtext. Am I supposed to be Nathaniel Devereaux's arm candy, or are these bouncy blondes just increasing their chances of getting the job by pushing their tits up and out in an attempt to catch his attention?

I look down at the black folder in my hands. It contains my life's work, recommendations from my last three bosses, and personal letters from college professors I TA'd for in college. I'm the only woman here with a folder. I'm also the only woman here who's eaten a carb in the last decade, but I think they might be proud of that one.

When I look back up I catch two girls looking away from me quickly and it makes my cheeks burn with embarrassment. I know that they're thinking I don't belong here. If you look around the room and pick out what doesn't fit in, it's me. But whatever they're whispering behind their perfectly manicured fingers doesn't make me get up and storm out, it just makes me straighten my posture.

They're right. I don't fit in here. I ate an entire bowl of pasta just last night and my scale says I'm creeping up on 150 lbs. My tits spill out of a bra if I'm not careful and I don't fit into any of those cute, overpriced, pieces of shit they sell at Victoria's Secret. I wear business skirts and fitted jackets because anything else makes me look like I'm trying to sell myself on a street corner. I don't fit in, I stand out because I'm not a waify model. And that's why I'm going to get the job.

"Ivy Scott," an older man calls from the doorway. He looks like Nathaniel Devereaux's father with his graying hair and warm smile.

I walk past the hungry pack of hyenas with my head held high. *Eat me, bitches*, I scream inside my head. "Hello," I return his smile. "I'm Ivy."

He leads me to a conference room that can seat a dozen comfortably. On the dark, mahogany table is a platter of scones, several bottles of mineral water, and napkins. "Ivy, your resume is quite impressive. In fact, one of your former employers is one of our current clients. We had the pleasure of reaching out to Mr. Grove and speaking to him about your employment."

He puts me at ease immediately. I cross my legs at the ankle and talk about my time working as Michael Grove's personal assistant. It doesn't surprise me that a man who works in the tech industry has a diverse financial portfolio and works with a financial investor, but it's delightful to find out that we have a small connection to build on.

The interview goes smoothly and by the end of it, I feel confident that I might actually secure this job. I'm sure those women in the waiting room have qualifications and connections of their own, but I have my fingers crossed that they're not as well-suited for this role as I am.

"Thank you for this opportunity," I shake Gregory's hand when we stand up. "It was wonderful to get to know more about the company and Mr. Devereaux's needs in a personal assistant."

Gregory's laugh is tinged with the faintest sense of irony. He grabs himself a mineral water and begins to lead me back toward the waiting room. "If you're offered this position, Miss Scott, I have to warn you that Nathaniel is a very charming man."

That's why there are a dozen long-legged blondes lined up outside, I want to say, but I bite my tongue and keep those words to myself. "Er, thanks for the warning?" I'm not sure how to respond anymore.

"I only tell you because he has a habit of flirting with his personal assistants. While he has a very specific type," Gregory looks back at me and eyes me quickly, "we are trying to make sure that we take that into account by hiring someone who won't fall for his charms and isn't litigious."

I don't fall for anyone's charms and, to be frank, I'm probably not Nathaniel Devereaux's type. "Sir, I can assure you that I am strictly professional." Google images brought up several photos of my potential boss wearing tinier girls than I on his arm at several charity events. I doubt that I'm the 'type' Gregory is talking about.

Gregory opens the door to the waiting room with the same warm smile on his face that he had before. "I'm happy to hear it, Miss Scott. We'll be in touch."

The waiting room is no longer filled with women. There must have been other people helping with the interview process other than Gregory. I walk through the silent room and wonder about this man who could possibly be my new boss. What did he do with other women? Has he been taken to court before? How charming is he really?

I guess none of this matters unless I get a callback from Gregory offering me the job. I might as well not hold my breath, either. Just in case.

24

NATHANIEL

The email from Gregory includes Ivy Scott's resume, which is impressive, to say the least. She's been a personal assistant since she graduated college five years ago, working for three different individuals. There's was a six-month stint where she was overlapping her time with two of them. That had to have been exhausting.

I hear a knock on my door and I tell the person to come in. "Hey there," Gregory announces with a genial smile, as per usual. "So how do you like Ivy? She seemed like the best of the lot in terms of experience."

"She's qualified, that's for sure," I say as my eyes continue to scan the two-page PDF he sent me. "Is she one of the agency girls?"

Gregory takes a seat in front of my desk and gives me one of his fatherly looks. "Look, Nate," and I can tell that a lecture is coming.

"Greg," I return his look with one of my own, pointed and stern, "I know what you're going to say, but whatever you're thinking, stop. It didn't go down like you think it did." Three personal assistants in the last two years have quit and attempted to sue the company due to me. Another couple left in tears, fired after they failed to do their job when our "relationship" fell apart.

"It's a sticky situation. Most of the girls who applied were agency girls." They were the ones who showed up on day one and were long gone before they made it to three months. "Ivy isn't from the agency. She's nothing like the agency girls, either. I think you'll like her though."

I didn't care if I'd like Ivy, as long as she did her job. In fact, the less I liked her and vice versa, the more likely our relationship would work out. And by a relationship I meant our working one. "As long as she can do the job, Greg. I don't care about anything else. I don't want anything else." Out of the five personal assistants who quit in the last two years, I only slept with one of them. I might have flirted with all of them, but that was harmless.

Gregory leans back in the chair and eyes me carefully. I turn my eyes back to my screen and continue to look at Ivy Scott's resume in hopes of diverting his attention.

I know what the company rumors are. I know what the girls in marketing say about me and what the guys working their way up in finance say, too. I know that I'm a good-looking man in my thirties that half the women want to be with and all the men want to be. I know who I am, but I also know who I'm not.

I'm not the playboy financial investor that the tabloids paint me out to be. I might make tech tycoons millions of dollars a year by investing their money right, but I don't do it to get the girls. I do it because I love the math behind it, the rush it gives me when I get it right. I'm a little nerdy at heart and there's nothing wrong with that.

"So what's this Ivy Scott even look like?" I ask after a few moments of silence.

"Nathaniel," Gregory says with a scolding tone to his voice.

I look away from my computer and shake my head at him. "Not because I'm interested in her," I tell him with a roll of my eyes, "but because the pack of wild animals out there will be." I work with a bunch of dogs, there's no doubt about that. I've been one of them a time or two, but I'm not as big a dog as they paint me out to be. I've got a type, but it isn't what they'd expect.

Gregory stands up and shakes his head back at me. "She's nothing you'd be interested in, Devereaux. Let's just stick with that."

We'll see, I think to myself. They'd be surprised to find out that my type isn't the kind of girl who would blow away in a strong wind.

25

IVY

Gregory calls me himself to offer me the job. His voice is practically beaming with excitement as he gives me the nitty-gritty details of salary negotiation, lunch break, and varying hours dependent upon Nathaniel Devereaux's busy schedule. "If you could start Monday, that would work perfectly."

Since I've been out of work for a week, Monday works great. "I appreciate you keeping me in mind, sir," I tell Gregory before I hang up the phone. This has been the best day of my life. In terms of pay, working for Nathaniel is going to be the best gig I've ever had. I'm not sure what type of exorbitant fee this guy requires to render his services, but he better be the best in the business. For what I'm making, he's probably raking in at least 10x this amount.

When I walk into the office on my first day of work, I try to look my best. I remember what all the girls from the interview did with their hair and outfits and try to replicate them with little success. My hair is curled and piled into a clip on the top of my head. My thicker body is poured into my usual business dress, though I let the neckline slip half an inch lower than usual, and I even wore a pair of high heels. But even feeling sexier than usual doesn't prepare me for what I walk in on.

Gregory leads me to my desk we both let out a sigh when we come across a suited up, broad-shouldered God sitting on the edge and entertaining no less than half a dozen leggy women who could pass for models. I'm not sure what Gregory's sigh means, but mine is pure frustration. He could have Captain America's ass and I still wouldn't want it to be parked on my soon-to-be desk.

"Hey, Nathaniel," Gregory greets his compatriot as we walk up, "this is your new assistant, Ivy Scott."

I can feel the envy radiating from the girls Nathaniel was just speaking to. Buckle up, ladies, I've been jealous of girls like you my entire life. If all you want is to spend up close and personal time with a man who looks like this, go right ahead. Believe me, I'm not stealing anything from you.

I shove a hand out toward my new boss and give him my sweetest smile. "Good morning, sir." I hope I don't sound too chipper.

He looks down at my outstretched hand and eyes it for a second before meeting it with his own. His fingers look more carefully manicured than mine, but I don't comment on it. "Nice to meet you, Ivy," Nathaniel says with a smile that stretches across his face. "I take it you know your way around an office?"

That singular question makes me wonder what kind of girls were hired to be his personal assistant before. "Um, well, I can figure out a broken printer, I know how to read, and if you need me to fetch you a latte, I can do that, too." My pluck makes that smile of his grow and my heart stops just a little. He's more handsome than I thought. With baby blue eyes looking me up and down and appreciation filling his gaze, this man might be trouble.

"I'll let you know if there's *anything* you can do for me, Ivy," he says with an undercurrent that sounds vaguely sexual.

I take a seat on the desk provided for me and fire up my computer. Fingers crossed that he's a busy man with plenty on his plate. If he's got time to flirt, then I'm going to be screwed. I can't afford to have a sexy, good-looking man like that look at me the way he just did. Even if he meant nothing by it, my vibrator does not have enough battery power to get me through the nights if he keeps that up.

26

NATHANIEL

I wasn't expecting Ivy, not in the least. She's a plus-size queen in a land where being thin is in. There's nothing wrong with a girl who takes care of herself and prides herself on a flat stomach, that just isn't my kind of girl.

I spend the day in my office trying to focus on paperwork and clients and I can't get the numbers to add up when my mind is too busy trying to figure out what to say to the girl sitting outside my office. Her eyes focus on her screen and never once flicker in my direction, and it kills me.

Is she not interested in me? Because I find that hard to believe. I'm a lot of women's type. In fact, I would go on to say that there are very few women out there that I couldn't have. I just have to take off my shirt and watch the ladies come running for a chance to feel my rock-hard abs. If they go a little lower, they'll feel a rock hard something else.

In the middle of my thoughts, there's a knock on my door and Ivy pokes her head in. "Hey, just wanted to see if there was anything I could help you with. Your eyebrows seem a little knit in frustration and I just want to offer my services."

So she has been watching me. How did I not catch her? No matter, she's offering her services now and this will allow me to get to know her a little better.

"Yes, sit," I gesture to the chairs in front of my desk. "We've got a few big clients we're onboarding right now and I've just been going over portfolios, determining what type of risk they want to take, if they—" but when I look up to finish speaking, though her eyes are intently taking in what I'm saying, I can read that she's not wholly invested. I'm talking financial shop and while she'll listen to me talk all day, it probably isn't her thing. "It's a lot," I finish.

Ivy smiles at me and sits on the edge of her chair. "Just tell me what you'd like me to do and I'm happy to help where I can."

I've been distracted by her all day, so the only thing she could do right now is tell me more about herself. "How about you order us some lunch and we take a break from all this?" I suggest as I lean back in my chair. "Gregory hired you and showed me your resume, but I'd like to get to know you a little better. I think a little team bonding over some sushi would be an excellent way to do that."

Her face lights up and she nearly pops right out of her chair. "I know the perfect place. It's a mom-and-pop sushi bar on 130th Street. I used to date their son, actually," she says with a fondness in her voice that strikes a strange feeling into my chest that I later identify as jealousy, "I'm sure they'll deliver!" Ivy gets my order and trails out of the room to order lunch, leaving me behind, flabbergasted.

If I were the one ordering lunch, I would have put 'sushi' into Google and picked the first restaurant to come up, assuming they didn't have bad reviews. But Ivy knows the little people, has a connection to them, and swears they'll be here within half an hour. I don't know how they'll do it, hell, I don't know how she does it, but I'm excited. I think the kids call these butterflies and I haven't felt them since I was in high school.

—

Ivy drives a Toyota Prius, not because she's environmentally conscious, but because her parents bought it for her years ago and she can't afford to upgrade her car. She lives with her two best friends, Ariel and a drag queen named Monroe. "Ariel and I haven't always been best friends, but after three years of sharing a bathroom, you become close."

I've never shared a bathroom with anyone a day in my life. Even here at the office, I have a private one just a few feet away. The perks of being wealthy, I suppose.

"Tell me about your best friends," she says as she expertly wields a pair of chopsticks.

What's there to say? Jonathan and I went to prep school together and thought we were going to change the world with renewable energy. Then we went to college. I went to Yale and he went to Stanford. "We talk once a week, text a lot, probably see one another every couple of months. I manage his financial portfolio and I've invested in his tech company out in Silicon Valley. He and his boyfriend are starting a family. Their surrogate is 7 months pregnant, I believe. He says I'm going to be named godfather, but we'll see."

This is the most exciting part for Ivy, who tells me with a face full of excitement that this is great news. "I love kids, but I don't want to have kids," she says with a guilty wince. "It's probably a horrible thing to say. All of my friends are reaching the years in their life where they have baby fever and are desperate to settle down and start families, but I'd be happy to be someone's godmother or fun aunt or something. I'm great with kids in small doses."

"No kidding. I've held my sister's kid three times since he was born and every single time there's been an incident with bodily fluids." Just thinking about it makes me shudder. "I didn't even know babies had that much poo inside of them."

Ivy practically cackles imagining what happened to me and I didn't even tell her. When she grabs her sides, in stitches with laughter, she's the most beautiful I've seen her yet.

I chance a glance at the clock and realize that almost two hours have passed since she walked into my office. It flew by in a fit of confessions and jokes, admissions and laughter at shared pain. I forgot for a minute that she was my assistant. "I like you, Ivy," I tell her after a moment, a smile hanging on my lips.

Her giggles stop almost immediately. "What?" She asks, a frown stitching its way onto her features.

That was something I meant to say to myself, but the words slipped out of my mouth. Instead of rushing to take them back, I shrug at her and say them again. "I like you."

She makes a quick determination about the road she should take and says, "I like you, too, Nathaniel. You seem like a nicer boss than I expected you to be." It seems like she's chosen to go the friendly route. That's fine, for now.

27

IVY

Nathaniel is an unexpected joy in the office. After that first day, he continues to maintain his genial air whenever he's around me. It doesn't hurt that he's not fake, either.

We get into a routine where we have lunch together on Fridays. He leaves it up to me. "Just make it somewhere small, like that sushi place we had on your first day. Expand my horizons, Ivy." And I make it my mission to sample culinary delights all over the city.

On those days we hole up in his office with boxes of takeout and paperwork strewn across his desk, intent on getting work done, but somehow never getting around to doing it.

Nathaniel tells me about who he is. He tells me about his socialite mother, who's spent her years all over the spectrum. Due to his antics in his sophomore year of high school, she was ostracized from social circles. He says this with a naughty grin. "There were nights she sat by my bedside and cried, asking me to do better and be a better person. But I was doing my rebel thing."

He turned his life around within six months, realizing that being a 'bad boy' was just a phase. But also because his father threatened to send him to military school, and Nathaniel had no desire to wake up at five in the morning. He'd be a saint ever since.

I responded tit for tat, sharing my all-time low moment in the summer after freshman year when I went to band camp and accidentally competed in a wet t-shirt contest. The boys loved it, but the other girls were jealous. I spent the rest of the summer being called 'Big Tits McGee' and other names that were meant to shame me. At that time in my life, they did.

"But now I'm pretty proud of the girls," I tell him with a mischievous smile. "Drinks are expensive, but I can go out with $5 and get drunk on a Friday with these girls." And this sends him into a fit of laughter. That doesn't mean I don't notice him checking out my tits to see if they do, indeed, reel in free drinks.

Our working relationship is just as in sync. I come in each day to find a folder on my desk from Nathaniel. It contains any paperwork I need to file for him, notes I need to take care of, and clients I need to check in on. In my inbox, I have forwarded emails to respond to for him. The rest of the day flows in a sundry of tasks that fill up the remainder of the hours.

Nathaniel is far from my most demanding employer. While the work is time-consuming in that it takes up each minute that I'm there, it's not so important that if a task doesn't get done today, the entire world will fall apart. Some things can be put off until tomorrow. Other things have to be done today. And he trusts me to make the right calls of what to finish today and what to finish tomorrow.

—

On this particular Thursday evening, I'm staying late. Gregory mentioned that there would be some flex time in my hours and that's perfectly fine. But as six melts into seven and seven disappears into eight, the sun has set and night in New York begins.

Lights in and around the office are going out as the usual late workers head home and even Nathaniel is heading out when he catches me sitting in front of my computer, fingers flying across the keyboard in an attempt to finish a final memo to a client about a recent loss.

"Hey, Ivy," he says with confusion written on his face. "What are you doing here this late?"

Usually, I'm never here past seven if I can help it. I've heard rumors about Nathaniel staying until the wee hours of the morning, but I chalk that up to him being a workaholic. "I'm almost done," I mumble without looking at him, "just one more paragraph."

He patiently waits for me to finish and fire off the email, a briefcase in his hands and his jacket strewn over it.

I start powering off my computer and let out a resounding sigh of relief. "Long day," I say with a nervous laugh. "I can lock up though if you want to go on ahead." I'm pretty sure that everyone on the floor has already left.

Nathaniel shakes his head in disagreement. "I'll wait. I can walk you to your car."

After two weeks ago my trusty Prius broke down. I took it in to the shop and they told me it would cost $3,000 in repairs. At fifteen years old, she wasn't even worth $3,000 anymore. "Oh, um," I hesitate, gathering my things, "that's okay."

He senses my hesitation and his patience turns into suspicion. "Ivy," Nathaniel says my name with all the fervor of a parent trying to suss out a guilty child, "what aren't you telling me?"

I've been carefully keeping my broken-down car out of our usual conversations. I didn't want him to feel bad for me, so I just didn't tell him about it. "It's not a big deal," I preface the story with a sigh, "but my Prius might be a little bit... broken." By the time I finish telling him what the repair person said, his eyes are practically bulging out of his head.

"How have you been getting to and from work these past couple of weeks?"

Not in a very charming sort of way, I think to myself. "The subway, usually," I grumble. "It's not a bad way to travel." I can hear the defensiveness in my voice.

Nathaniel purses his lips and then nods his head. "Alrighty then. Grab your things." He nods his head in the general direction of my items. "I'll take you home."

This was exactly what I was afraid of. I don't want his pity. I'm actually beginning to like him. The last thing I want is for him to feel bad for me. "No, Nathaniel, I—"

"You can grab your things or I can," he says with a shrug. "I'm amenable to either of these options. Just let me know which one you prefer and I'm happy to oblige."

His tone takes on his usual, professional, workplace demeanor and I know that there's no arguing with this man. "I'll get my things." I'll roll my eyes and gather up my belongings. "You're so testy this evening."

Nathaniel responds with a roll of his own eyes. "You would be too if you found out your favorite personal assistant was putting her life at risk riding the subway in the middle of the night."

I look at my watch to check the time. "It's 8:30."

He frowns and looks at his own watch. "Huh, look at that." Then he starts walking to the elevator. "You coming?"

Nathaniel is an enigma. He's funny and his upbringing was wildly different from my own. We live lives that are practically perpendicular to one another and I know there's talk around the office of why we're so buddy-buddy. But Nathaniel is a good guy. He cares for the people he works with. He wants to get to know them and see them do well.

He's also incredibly sexy, so there's that, too.

28

NATHANIEL

I anticipated dropping Ivy off at her building and driving home, but she's been unexpected since the beginning.

"Hey. Want to come up and have dinner with Ariel, Monroe, and I?" She waves her phone and me and reassures me that she's already asked her roommates. "It won't be long. Monroe is about to go to a gig downtown and Ariel's boyfriend, Beau, is about to get off work here in about an hour. But they made lasagna and there's plenty to share if you're interested."

How can I resist that beautiful smile that spreads across her lips and invites me in? "I can't remember the last time I had lasagna." As I say those words, my stomach growls in anticipation.

"Monroe has a lactose sensitivity and usually has to pop a couple of Lactaid pills before we eat, but he's also the one who packs five kinds of cheese into the lasagna. So I hope that's okay." She climbs out of my car with my eyes on her ass. Five kinds of cheese, huh? "He likes to say it's his grandmother's recipe, too, but she's a nice lady from Kansas. The closest she's ever been to Italian is the aisle at her local Kroger."

Her building has an elevator, but Ivy counsels me against using it. "I've been stuck on there at least three times in the last six months. I think there's something wrong with the electrical panel. It passed inspection, but I refuse to use it anymore. The four flights up to our apartment aren't bad anyway." But that's coming from a woman who does it every day.

I may work out daily, but I'm not prepared for four flights in business loafers. No wonder her ass looks so good. If she's climbing these stairs day-in and day-out, I would expect nothing less. "I may have to stay the night," I say in a huff when we finally reach the fourth floor, "I'm not sure I'm going to be able to make it back down."

Ivy chuckles and leads me down the hallway to her apartment. "After you try Monroe's lasagna, we'll be able to roll you down the stairs. Trust me."

I can smell the red sauce before she opens the door. It's heavenly out here. Her apartment is a barrage of noise when we step inside. Though the living room is immaculate, there is a steady stream of sound coming from every direction.

In the kitchen someone is washing dishes, singing loudly to Miley Cyrus. From the hallway where the bedrooms presumably are is another country heard from in the way of Justin Bieber. A bathroom light is on and you can hear the faint sounds of another artist playing from another speaker. The smell of lasagna and garlic bread assault my senses.

"Sorry about the noise," Ivy yells over all the music and singing, "gimme a minute!" And in under sixty seconds, she's shut everything down. I hear exchange words with Monroe in the kitchen as she turns off the music and tells him she has a guest. Then she makes her way to the bathroom, flips off the music, and turns off the light. Crossing the hall she goes into what I assume is Ariel's room and in hushed tones tells her that I'm here for dinner and turn off the music. Then all of a sudden everyone is popping around corners to eye me up and down.

"Hi," I say with an awkward smile. I stand there in two pieces of a three-piece suit, my jacket still in the car. "I'm Nate."

Monroe screams. "Hon-nee!" He claps his soapy hands together. "I hope you like lasagna. I tried a new cheese tonight. We're a six-layer family now!"

And I don't know if I'm excited or scared, but Ivy shakes her head. "Babe, remember what I told you," she reminds him, "we use our inside voices when we have company."

Babe? Are they dating? I feel like I shouldn't have to worry about Monroe because he's four inches shorter than me and wears his hair in a military buzzcut, but maybe that's Ivy's type. She hasn't been really indicative of what's going on in her personal life.

"Ten minutes until dinner!" Monroe doesn't listen to Ivy in the slightest. "I call dibs on sitting next to tall, dark, and scrumptious!"

Huh. Maybe they aren't dating. Maybe they just have the same taste in men...

29

IVY

Monroe can be an overwhelming personality sometimes, but Nathaniel takes it in stride. It helps that Ariel pulls out what she calls her stash of "lasagna wine".

"You can't have lasagna without pairing it with a red," she says as she pours all of us a heaping glass of Cabernet. "You're all a bunch of uncultured swine." Her piercing green eyes turn to Nathaniel and she flashes him a smile, "Not you, of course. You didn't know the rules. Next time though, I will include you in all sweeping phrases."

They do their best to break him in gently, but that's not saying much. Monroe talks about the latest threesome he's been in, Ariel discusses whether or not she's going to kill her boyfriend if he doesn't propose, and I casually shoot glances at Nathaniel while trying to determine if he wants to run away screaming.

"I keep telling him that I'm not getting any younger," Ariel insists as she pours Nathaniel and I another glass of wine, topping off our third glass each. "But he keeps saying he wants to save up for a ring. I don't care if it's giant or anything. I just want to be with him forever."

She's going to be wine drunk by the time that precious fool gets off work if we don't cut her off. I stand up and lean over my boss. "Excuse me," I say with a nervous chuckle, "just gonna grab this," I say as I snatch the glass from in front of Ariel.

"Hey!" She yells.

"Baby girl," Monroe's eyes widen as he looks from Ariel and then over to me, "you better run. You are bigger than her, but I bet she will—oh!" He is taken aback when I start drinking Ariel's glass of wine, holding my hand up to hold off our cranky roommate.

Nathaniel, who's been relatively silent, snorts.

With half the glass down, I stop to take a breath. "Ariel, don't make me drink this whole glass. I will if I have to, but don't make me. If you drink anymore, you're going to show up at Beau's place shit-faced and ready to call up Monroe for a threesome." "Hell yeah, girl," he says with a smile, "let her have that glass, then. I'd fuck the both of ya," Monroe gives Ariel a wink.

I round on him with a heavy glare. "And you, Monroe, shut up. I thought with my boss here that you might calm down a little, but you're outdoing yourself, truly. That little information about what to do with your pinky and a man's asshole was riveting, but was it necessary?"

Realization doesn't even dawn on him. "You can do that to a woman too, you know," Monroe stares blankly at me. "I actually found out about it when I was with Jasmine, this stripper from—"

I hold my hand up. "Enough," I yell, silencing the chaos that is my home life. "I'll clean up. If you're all done for the evening, feel free to depart and go your separate ways. Thank you for introducing yourselves to Nate. I'm sure this is an evening he won't forget."

So much for prim and proper Ivy Scott, his personal assistant who knows how to manipulate every program in the Microsoft Suite and is food cultured beyond compare. He's probably counting down the seconds until he can run screaming down those stairs and drive back to his high-rise condo on the upper east side where nights like tonight don't happen.

—

It doesn't take long for Monroe and Ariel to say their goodbyes and flee the scene of the crime. I'm dishing up lasagna into Tupperware containers for all of us to take to work in the upcoming days when Nathaniel comes into our small, 2-person kitchen and leans up against the counter. "Wow, you sure know how to command a room," he says with a smile. "I should let you loose on some of the board meetings I have to attend at the office. You would put some of the guys in check."

He's just trying to make me feel better, and it works. "Putting up with those two has given me the ability to handle anything." The words come off in a light-hearted sort of way, but I feel a little embarrassed about tonight. I didn't want them to sound as crass as they did, or to get that drunk, or require me to act as the middleman.

"In all these weeks we've spent getting to know one another, tonight really gave me a better idea of who Ivy Scott really is."

Great. Here it is. You're fired, Ivy Scott. You're not good enough for my office. Ivy Scott. You're just not the kind of girl I want being my personal assistant, Ivy Scott.

"And I have to say, I really, really like her."

I almost drop the glass lasagna dish in the sink. "What?" The word slips out sharp and unsteady.

"You're impossibly smart, more so than half the men in the office. And you have this intuition about checking in on me. I don't know if you can see me looking puzzled or have this sixth sense or what, but you always come in to offer help when I need a distraction the most."

He pushes off the counter and comes closer to me. "You've ingrained yourself into my life, to the point where I look forward to coming to work just to see you. I live for our Friday lunches because you're always picking new and interesting places for us to try, then we spend hours just talking about life and who we are. I haven't felt that way with someone since before college."

My heart starts fluttering at the way he talks. I knew that what we were doing was verging on some sort of relationship territory, but I thought he looked at me like a friend, someone who he confided in but didn't want to sleep with. I wanted more, sure, but I didn't think he saw me like that.

"And I thought you were beautiful the first day that I saw you, but every day since has been like watching a flower slowly blossom. You've opened up to me, showed me who you really are, and it's gotten under my skin. I don't even look at other women anymore because yours is the only face I see. When I'm awake, in my dreams, when I'm walking down the street."

He steps forward again, his body brushing against mine. "I can't help myself anymore, Ivy. I want to see if there's something between us."

Then he covers the space between us until I'm pushed up against the wall and his body is molded into mine. His mouth covers mine, devouring my essence with a soul-stealing kiss.

For a fraction of a second I want to break away and tell him that we shouldn't do this, that this is wrong, but that melts away when his tongue slips past my lips and begins a passionate dance with mine.

30

NATHANIEL

Ivy wraps her arms around my neck, slipping into desire and need.

I find myself running my hands over her body and searching for the hem of her shirt, desperate to pull it over her head. I know that I shouldn't go any further, but I can't stop myself. I finally have this beautiful, curvy woman in my hands and I want her, all of her.

Shirt pulled off and discarded on the kitchen counter, Ivy's body presses against me in a thin bra and skirt. I lean down between her succulent breasts, pull back the sheer bra, and envelope one of her nipples in my hot, wet mouth. I swirl my tongue around the nipple until it becomes a hard, stiff bud and Ivy is moaning for more.

I run my hand down her thigh and feel between her legs. Heat radiates from her pussy, she wants this just as much as I do, but I should ask first. What we're doing is a recipe for disaster at work. I'm making all the rumors come true.

I break away from Ivy's nipple and re-cover it with the lace of her bra. "Is it okay if we continue?" I ask nearly breathless with lust for her.

Ivy's eyes are wild with her own pleasure waiting to be sated. "Yes," she says immediately. "Please." This second word comes at the tail end of the first and is spoken with desperation.

I would do anything for her right now.

I fall to my knees in front of her and help pull down her skirt. Ivy slides down the zipper and I slip it off. I'm rewarded with the sight of her curvaceous bottom in a thong, which I'm only too happy to remove if it means coming face-to-face with her sweet pussy.

That glorious sight is already dripping with wetness. With her legs spread apart, I start by taking long, glorious licks of her, devouring her sweetness. Ivy's fingers get lost in my hair as she moans. I wish I was doing this in a bed where she could be more comfortable, but this is where we are and I don't want to break the spell of what we have.

Ivy gasps when I slip a finger inside of her, followed by a second. The hand she has curled in my hair only tightens on my locks, pulling my face closer toward her button. I use my free hand to travel up her body and grab one of her breasts. My tongue lolls around her clit and her body writhes against my touches.

She is sweet beyond measure when she starts screaming my name and bucking against my face, her body trembling with orgasm. Her fingers nearly rip the hair out of my head, but I would happily take that risk every day to relive this moment for the rest of my life.

When I pull away from her still shuddering body, I'm throbbing in my slacks. I have to have her, fully and completely. "Where's your room?" I ask from the floor, still on my knees.

Ivy bites her lip to keep from smiling, "All the way to the back and left."

I spring up from my position on the ground and grab her hand, leading her toward her bedroom as quickly as I can. I don't take in the elements of her personality just yet because I want her to take me in, every inch of me.

Ivy climbs on the bed as I quickly disrobe. When I pull my boxer briefs down, I look up just in time to see her eyes widen and her lips form the words 'holy shit'. Words that I've come to know quite well in reference to my size.

"I'm going to make you scream my name again," I promise her as I climb on the bed, crawling between her thick, cushy thighs. One day I want to have those wrapped around my ears as she rides my face. Maybe even later tonight.

Without prompting, Ivy wraps her legs around my waist as I escort my erect cock toward her entrance. Her body arches as I slip inside her wet pussy. Nails that I never realized she had rake across my back in response to my thick, hard member filling her up. She's tight and slick, but her legs wrapped around me invite me deeper inside of her.

I rock my hips back and forth, finding a rhythm that works for both of us. Ivy finds a similar pattern of thrusting her hips up to meet mine, moaning when my cock hits her tight center.

I can see the next fifty years of my life with this woman and that's all it takes for the both of us to tumble over the edge.

Ivy's pussy throbs with her orgasm, gripping my cock as she swears to God and makes me wonder how religious she is. With my member deep inside of her, my own pleasure rips through me like a flash burn. Her pulsating pussy milks me for every drop of my seed as the two of us share the most intimate of moments.

I fall onto the bed beside her, muscles tense and my body physically exhausted from the day. Between work and play, I'm ready to sleep. But with Ivy beside me, I would rather just watch her all night.

"What now?" She asks as she turns her head to face me.

"Round... three?" I ask, doing the math in my head. For her, it would be a third orgasm, and I'm okay with that.

Ivy grins and rolls her eyes. "No, not *that*. I mean this, between us. I've heard the office rumors about you. Do I need to worry about you dropping me like a hot potato?"

I wondered how much she heard around the office. All those rumors would come out eventually, but I guess now I'd have to nip them in the bud with her. "I didn't sleep with those girls, Ivy. One of them, yeah, but not the others. I didn't even have lunch with them the way I have with you. It was just a case of one-sided affection that they took too far. I'm a very in-demand kind of man."

There she goes rolling her eyes again. I want to lean over and kiss her. "I'm serious though. I can't tell anyone I'm sleeping with my boss. They would laugh at me. And half those girls would claw my eyes out."

I couldn't care less, honestly. "Tell them you're dating your boss then," I suggest. "And if anyone gives you any grief, send them my way."

Ivy thinks about this in silence for several minutes, long enough to make me nervous. But just before I'm about to ask her if everything is okay, she says, "Dating, huh? Like, boyfriend and girlfriend?"

The labels remind me of high school. They take me back to an easier time when I didn't have to worry about HR getting involved and corporate lawyers making us sign contracts that insisted we wouldn't sue the company for wrongful termination if our relationship ended and then we were fired, coincidentally, of course. It would never be intentional.

But Ivy might be worth the hassle and the extra paperwork. It'll take up half of my Friday afternoon and I'll get razzed by the guys on the top floor, especially Gregory, but I'm not sure what else we can do. "We can call each other whatever we'd like, Ivy."

"How about peanut butter and jelly?" She says, challenging my 'whatever we'd like' philosophy.

I'd rather die than go back on my work. "Alright, you tell anyone that asks that you're my jelly. Sound good to you?"

The smile on Ivy's face tells me I made the right decision. "Sounds good to me, peanut butter."

It definitely feels like I'm back in high school now, and that's perfectly okay with me.

www.ingramcontent.com/pod-product-compliance
Lightning Source LLC
Chambersburg PA
CBHW071122261125
36008CB00018B/154